P9-CDG-712

The Mastery of You

Renu S. Persaud

Published by Waldorf Publishing
2140 Hall Johnson Road
#102-345
Grapevine, Texas 76051
www.WaldorfPublishing.com

The Mastery of You

ISBN: 978-1-944784-83-6
Library of Congress Control Number: 2016957067

Copyright © 2017

All rights reserved. No part of this book may be reproduced or transmitted in any form or by any means whatsoever without express written permission from the author, except in the case of brief quotations embodied in critical articles and reviews. Please refer all pertinent questions to the publisher. All rights reserved. No part of this book may be reproduced or transmitted in any form or by any means, electronic or mechanical, including photocopying, recording, or by an information storage and retrieval system except by a reviewer who may quote brief passages in a review to be printed in a magazine or newspaper without permission in writing from the publisher.

Dedication

To Sarah, Emma and David

Affectionately, my soul is encased by a triumvirate, together, we are one.

..with all my Love..

Disclaimer

Certain names and identifying details have been changed to protect the privacy of individuals.

I have tried to recreate events, locales, and conversations from my memories of them. In order to maintain anonymity, in some instances I have changed the names of individuals and places; I may have changed some identifying characteristics and details such as physical locales, occupations, and places of residence.

Table of Contents

Chapter One: What Is the Meaning of Self-Mastery?...1

Chapter Two: The Paradox of Selfishness...34

Chapter Three: Self-Reflection and Self-Mastery...103

Chapter Four: The Art of You...139

Chapter Five: The Social Butterfly Effect...167

Chapter Six: The Power of Self-Mastery...186

Chapter Seven: The Self-Mastered Artist...225

Chapter Eight: The Kindness Revolution...253

Acknowledgments...283

Author Biography...285

Index...286

Preface

The Mastery of You is not an overnight creation. Indeed, I questioned this undertaking many times. Ultimately, I persevered. I thank you for reading my book, and I sincerely hope you enjoy reflecting upon the subject of your *Self.* Most importantly, I share with you an intimate picture of my life, my personal and scholarly experiences.

Henceforth, the knowledge that elucidates this book is complex. I evoke moments in my existence that have created happiness, fulfillment, sadness, fear, anguish, sorrow, love, hate, remorse, and pride. These are bound by the golden thread of my experiences and scholarly work; they are a compilation of who I am today.

In synthesis, these features created a compelling path toward self-mastery which I wholeheartedly share with you. One does not disrupt one's life to practice self-mastery; it is interwoven in everyday practice.

To unconditionally practice the mastery of you means your interactions are guided by the realization that you understand from your own and *the* other's viewpoint, and this transpires after you have engaged with and have an appreciation of your own thoughts first. *By nurturing* you, *you reap the rewards of treating others with respect and dignity.* I refer to this as the *Paradox of Selfishness* (discussed in chapter two.) This is what the mastery of self allows you to do—you must care for you so that you can care for others and ultimately for humanity.

Driven by my scholarly work at the University of Toronto and today as a professor, my investigation stems from interaction and notations with thousands of people and students over the years. My writing emanates from my observations about social life, cultural values, and selfhood.

To write these pages, I had an infinite amount of material to fuse together. I performed a detailed literature review, and I researched sociological, psychological, philosophical, art, cultural, historical, business, and neuroscientific sources. This enabled me to develop a cross-disciplinary analysis regarding the elements required for self-mastery. My own research was analyzed in relation to other studies of self-worth and personal success.

Having found a correlation between sense of self, personal and professional fulfillment, and lifelong success, I demonstrate how self-mastery precedes and ultimately shapes our self-worth.

My observations and humble wisdom are meant to be shared by everyone, whether you are a parent, entrepreneur, CEO, or professional. We can all learn the mastery of self at any point in our lives because it is a cumulative practice. We must master our own abilities, and then, when we care for others, we want them to do the same.

To make the most of these pages, I request you have a thought-provoking internal dialogue with yourself *during* your interactions with others. You must contemplate: *Did I make that person feel worthy? Did I put myself in their shoes?* Self-mastery enlivens and naturally guides your interactions by this thought process.

Time, I want you not, no more. Leave me, free me.

Disguise your stifling presence,

You stand before me, behind me, beside me, above me, beneath me and from within.

You catch the fragile only.

Petals pink and green fall forever.

Permanently grounded, time encases me as my captor dying to ascend upon my soul.

–Renu S. Persaud

Chapter One, Summary: The chapter begins with a personal vignette. My journey of sacrifice from early on transcends to my role as a mother which only intensified the sentiment of giving. I then recall a time when a few weeks spent in the Northern region of India created a courageous path for my entire life. I realized that self-betrayal was the result of my own relentless need for acceptance. This awareness altered my outlook about life, forever. My loneliness from self-betrayal transformed to an intense sense of not-belonging; a sentiment that eventually changed to self-regard and freedom from my own practice of self-mastery. Thus, self-mastery becomes a practical tool for enriching our lives. Indeed, it can be formulated from self-analysis and theoretical assumptions into practice.

What Is the Meaning of Self-Mastery?
My Personal Path: An Exploration of Self
June, 2009

Piercing through the window pane, the flashes of sunlight soaked through the ruby-red velvet curtains. It was 2 p.m. The calm of waking in the sun-drenched slumber of late afternoon absorbed me.

A sleeping angel in my arms—I marveled at her translucent, silken touch.

Faithfully, upon waking, she was the first to beckon my somnolent eyes; her tender breaths always more tantalizing to my ears even as Brahms' lullaby played on repeat. Hidden from sight and clenched in her mellifluous, consoling grasp, my baby finger was tenderly secured. I often wondered—was she protecting me, or I her?

As the days submerged to nights, my presence was in disarray.

I felt absorbed in a bizarre rapture. I became one with my child as I have done with those I care for in my life. Self-sacrificing, I desired to be the best mother, wife, daughter, and professor. Still, my desires were not selfless, but laden with self-interest.

I realized my giving was guided by the desire for adulation. My life was consumed with the disdainful pursuit of exaltation, and a numbing lament consumed me. I had fallen into an obscure oubliette yearning to fulfill my roles with exemplary kindness.

I was torn.

As intense days of unhappiness set in, I became lost. Reality had vanished into a thin veil of splintered existence; my sustenance was missing.

I desperately desired to *be* selfish. I could no longer be compelled to give selflessly by a misguided euphoric need for veneration.

I heard the ringing of the doorbell.

Too weary to look, speak, or exist with anyone, I ignored it. Looking through the imposing yet opaque windows of the bedroom with ceilings so high it felt empty, I saw the Joe's Gourmet Foods truck. It reversed down the heavily stoned driveway. I blankly gazed as they curbed out of sight.

Unrelentingly, Joe and his wife Mary would deliver fresh foods to clients every Tuesday, a service I became easily accustomed to for the wrong reasons. Sometimes, they were the only people I interacted with for the week or month.

In a broken moment, my want for a baneful nonexistence unraveled a hopeless dismay. Nothingness consumed me in anguish, torment, fear, and sorrow. Mechanically I became the muse of my self-inflicted torment. Taunted by the compulsion to unchain my soul, I departed on my journey of self-recovery by self-mastery.

Here is my story.

September, 2001

The summer breeze turned cool and days became darker sooner; autumn was on the horizon. I remembered this time well but only after I tried desperately to forget.

I often wondered if this fragmented memory was purely a dream or an actual sentient experience. Do you have those moments in your life where your reality becomes so blurred and distorted it appears to have fallen into the realm of reveries? I believe if the authentic experience was too painful to remain real, relegating it to the demesne of dreams somehow hindered the pain from mutating.

The smoldering clouds in my consciousness did not allow me to discern. Yet, despairingly in my heart, I knew it was real—I merely wished it away, as a dream.

November 2001, Kausani

The heavens of Kausani completed their descent upon my mind, resonant with an oblivious dismal grace. The self-destructive splendor enthralled me to a place I have never known again. A serendipitous search rendered my spirit lost.

I stood amid peaks veiled in mist as the mountains impressed upon the sky above. Beneath, the emerald green pines embraced the blue abyss. Valleys swirled in between jagged glacial plains as the hills of jade touched everything.

Kausani is a tourist haven, one of the nearest points surrounding the Himalayan escarpment. The snow-laced turquoise mountain terrain beckoned to me a bitter serenity, a magnificence that time after time disquieted me, was foreboding.

Alpine glaciers hard against soaring gorges were cloaked in an unrelenting and silent strength.

Arms outstretched, I felt I could touch the imposing vale.

Descending in this abode of snow, far away from modernity, I felt a detached calmness. The soaring and stiff stillness created a landscape, claiming the backdrop for which my life was to unfold before me.

Life is strange; I was surrounded by the most beautiful scene my eyes had embraced, and I was living through the unhappiest moments of my life.

I had no choice but to daringly surrender myself each day to the company of this virulent tranquility. My disarrayed existence meant my days were absorbed into the nightfall and the nights muddled into dimness.

Yet I felt a rare perpetual connection to myself more than any other moment in my life. Why? I wondered. The answer was simple. I could *be* completely with me.

The only discreet disturbance was when the innkeeper soundlessly entered the green wooden door at the end of the concrete and pine archway. With misty blue eyes that matched the mountains, he would pace into my stony cold villa, which was always lit with a natural wood-burning fireplace.

Still handsome in his wrinkled encasing, with strong muscular arms that did not match his age, he never looked in my eyes.

He always wore a beige angora hat. A woven gray and dotted red scarf was often draped around his neck. He brought me trays with sweets or a meal for one that fared more like a feast.

One cool and balmy afternoon, he entered the room with two copper gold-rimmed plates. The first plate was dressed with delicious confections, and on the other tray sat an old-fashioned silver teapot.

This familiar stranger was the only person I had known for weeks. Glancing down with reverence, he placed the salver before me, and silently was gone.

A morose serenity surrounded me. Oceans away, memories of my other beautiful life had turned to bitterness only a month ago.

The dust of my journey settled softly, never to be swept away. They were moments I forgot to remember in all the chaos of my life.

In this brazen land of calm, breathing in the pleasant sorrow of the Kashmiri air, my mind often wandered across the massifs to my Canadian existence. I sensed my father could feel my suffering.

He imagined the tears twinkling down the life-sized portrait of me now cut in half by secrets scattered among the ruins of being. My house would radiate with fragrant smells. The fusion of sandalwood incense, camphor, and nutmeg often danced together in my thoughts. Clarified butter and sugar added to the sweetness of the atmosphere at my vibrant, always lively Canadian home–a place that seemed a lifetime away.

October, 1998

Jaipur was bustling. The Pink City was pleasantly hazy with clamor. The noise of scooters packed the air with their ragged engines. Bollywood music played in the background as we walked by a busy paan café, he and I, side by side.

Colors in every vibrant tint imaginable were found everywhere, and dotted the lively paths.

Shops were scented with fragrant jasmine. Garlands of orange marigolds festooned the musky streets.

Apart from a yellow Tata cab here and there, the flamboyant rickshaws were a favored means of transportation. Each driver competed with the other for the most ostentatious decor to set their rickshaw apart as they hoped for the next customer. It was a greater accomplishment if a customer was a foreigner. They sought out foreigners and used a template for searching them out.

The drivers followed a code of conduct that included driving recklessly, singing randomly in a Shah Rukh style, and impatience was a virtue.

I beckoned to have a ride in a rickshaw; it looked amusing. I was rebuked tersely. A journey in an articulated vehicle was beneath me. I had to remain in the Cadillac with the driver when I was not accompanied by a chaperone, which was never.

Under no circumstances was I to set my precious golden-anklet slipper-wearing painted red toes in a rickshaw. My insistence for the rickshaw excitement rendered me complacent. I wanted to be bounced along on the sandy, gritty roads as the other normal mortals. To amend the denial of my request, I would later be taken on an evening joy ride on a Harley Davidson motorcycle, riding into the dusk, as if on an eventide.

Blowing horns in unison while playing the latest Bollywood song, drivers ricocheted their passengers to any destination. There was an indescribable life and excitement in the pink air as couples, business people, royalty, and students of the upper castes completed their day's deeds. Glancing into a sari store, I could see a young bride accompanied by her father, brothers, and about twelve other women.

They were selecting her wedding attire. She seemed immersed on a pyre, surrounded by ocean waves of layers upon layers of brocade, chiffon, taffeta, georgette, jacquard, polyester, and silk-charmeuse fabrication.

I would have felt stifled, bound by this showcase of such celebratory attention.

Twelve solid gold bangles encased in rubies and diamonds jangled happily on each of her mother's wrists. I felt a mix of anger and sorrow for this woman, who was oblivious to the repressive backdrop of her daughter's future.

I wondered if the mother had even contemplated how *her* daughter would exist after the glowing celebration. Surely, she was dimly aware.

Selecting the fineries and materials for the wedding seemed to hold a greater purpose and celebratory appeal than the actual sentient event. After all, her child was still hers, for now. I could not imagine how daunting the bride's decision would be.

Lingering flashes of a wedding still fresh in my mind, only weeks ago, impressed upon me, so close yet so far away. For a moment, I forgot I was a foreigner, but the people remembered to remind me by their glares, stares, elongated looks, whispers, and gasps.

I could not feel more uneasiness. Being thrust in this bustling environment was an act of compelling means. I had to visit the family who was royalty steeped from a Thakur lineage.

The palatial dwelling was on a main road in Rajasthan's capital. I stuck out as a numb limb. I tried desperately to dissolve into the atmosphere.

I could not.

My presence was glaring. My skin was light, my features were "Western," and I wore dresses.

My gestures, my posture, my walk, my confidence, my disposition, my jewelry (I refused to wear "real" everything,) and my hairstyle were contemporary. After all, I *was* bred in the West, and this became my greatest sin.

I declined to "conceal" my head, and this further abridged me to foreign status.

I knew only English, and when I spoke, people ran to me for autographs, believing I was a foreign "star."

Indeed, I felt like a star for the wrong reason, far away, dulled into the night sky—with all brightness of light, depraved. Merely being a "foreigner" rendered me celebrity status in these parts. It was strange, yet not odd. I felt an acrimonious and bitter happiness to have experienced a place I would never forget.

I couldn't realize this, then.

My bedroom was on the top floor, with a rooftop balcony. I stood looking over the gilded rail, which gave me the feeling I was imprisoned. Mostly alone, I observed the maid working.

Rajasthan was sandy, with desert-like surroundings; one of the maid's tasks was to clean the gritty particles that settled on furniture. This meant she dusted daily. She was content to enslave herself to servitude as her mother, grandmother, and great-grandmother had before her. Later, as she swept the garden, I watched from above the courtyard.

Her red glass bangles danced and clamored up and down both her tarnished wrists, tainted even at seventeen. The melody of the humming circles seemed to inspire her mundane work at hand.

I came to know of the days she wore plastic bangles because I missed the musical vibration of these circles of infinity. In spite of her repressors, she took pride in dressing herself and changed her bangles every day. I was her friend, if only in my mind.

She couldn't know.

I was permitted "never" to look at her, not even in her direction. If I did, it would bring a curse and devastation to the family honor. My endeavoring to act with any gesture of kindness meant *she* would be punished severely.

This consumed me.

I wished to give her every belonging of ardent material wealth, exquisite and hollow materials thrust upon me, so she could stop working and go to school.

One day, I fortuitously walked into the garden, her figure enthralled in the bed of earth as she sat trimming dead leaves from the amaryllis lilies, marigolds, orchids, and amaranth flower plants.

The attar beckoned my entry to the garden. Barefoot, I walked toward the jasmine tree, white petals blooming with fragrance. I handpicked a fragrant flower. Oblivious, I *was* aware of her presence, but she was scolded for not seeing me.

It was *her* fault.

She was an untouchable. It was utterly impure for me if she was in my presence.

This was unthinkable, yet I let it happen. I wanted to demonstrate, if only to myself, there was no effect on my "purity" whatsoever. I even tried to scientifically explain this using the laws of karma, laws of universality, evolution, biology, physiology, and plain logic.

I severely lost this battle even though my pureness was never threatened. I believed I knew the practices, the ideologies around "untouchables," but I was wrong—I was ignorant and unaware.

In her defense, I lamely told an elder the garden was not a room; it was outside, a part of nature. My desperate riposte was in vain.

As the day's sun was high, only women were home and there was no translator. I could barely express my feelings except in English, so nobody understood me. The household blamed the maid for my deliberate mistake.

The guilt was soul-scorching. I later asked *why* there existed such deference toward a fellow human being and demanded an explanation. This was perhaps the only time I demanded anything. It was explained we *are* the fortunate ones because our karma in our past life was virtuous. They have sown the seeds of their dejection in a previous life. Their suffering was their karmic fault, end of story.

My young mind did not allow me to apprehend. I began to question my own karma. While seemingly fortunate, I must have committed bad deeds in a previous life for my then-present reality. Pity for her destitution fueled my resentment on so many levels. I became distraught at humanity, at inequality and prejudice, for her lack of freedom, for her isolation.

I was angry for being Brahmin, and for him being of the royal caste. Somehow, I felt responsible for her despair. That night, I expressed my grief at this unfairness that I could not comprehend. I was told, "You will *learn* to be repulsed by their ilk."

How could I, a Canadian "girl," be given consideration by this culture? I often heard stories of foreigners immigrating to Canada, never to feel equal or accepted by our Canadian society. Now, in this new culture, I, a Canadian of status and position, felt beneath everything.

Frustration fueled my own reality. How could rejection harbor such contempt for fellow humans? For my thoughts alone, I knew I too would *never* belong.

Each day, the young maid arose at 4 a.m. Her hair was perfectly parted with a marooned red line down the middle of her forehead. With her head covered in a green scarf, her first task was to sweep the steps. The scratching of the natural broomstick fibers against concrete would awaken me very early, even before the yellow shadows of dawn.

There was a pervasive morose quality about her.

I could tell she was intelligent. I wished she could go to school. I could sense her yearning for knowledge. I'm sure this would have been her choice, if she had one.

I observed her love for learning in stolen moments. Inquisitively, she opened books as she cleaned the library. I knew this was her favorite part of the day, because the only

12

time I beheld her smile was once when she opened a book titled *Poems by Rumi*.

I still ponder how these two months of my life folded into an entire lifetime of questions. Certain questions will never be answered.

I would lie on a smothering bed, watching the ceiling fan spin, wondering what I was doing so far from home. I daydreamed of opening the heavy copper bolt and disappearing through it in the middle of night. There was a long stairway that connected the upper garden, bottom floors, and courtyard of the manor. I would have to walk past the room of his mother as I made my way down. I worried my shadow would be seen. Even if I climbed down, where would I have gone at midnight? It was a torturous thought. I wanted to escape desperately, but I was told stories about dacoits who roamed the streets looking for "kinds" like me.

I spent most of my days in this room, looking outside through the iron-barred windows. The house clamored with brothers, wives, and children. His younger brother was very close to him and known as the "young prince." He was married to a charming lady, Mina from Nainital, a northern hill station.

She could not bear children. Her guilt of disappointing the family meant she was tolerant and accepting of all things.

It was her suggestion we visit the northern region. The trip would allow her to see her parents, and I could experience one of the most beautiful places in the world.

Knowing Mina lived twelve hours away from her family, and it had been a year since she last saw them, made me feel rueful that I missed mine so tirelessly after only a few weeks.

We took an overnight coach, inner city jet, then finally a bus to make our ascent to the north. In a huge Tata bus, the ride for four and a driver seemed endless. We jolted around and around the steep and submerging valley.

I felt as though I was ascending toward the heavens. Selfishly, I desperately desired for the bus to roll over. I wanted to freely descend into the vapors of the valley.

Mina's family had a beautiful welcome for us.

Upon arrival, the keepers took our bags inside the rose-colored cement house. After the obligatory introductions, I asked for coffee. I was unsure if my request was odd. Unlike Canada, where coffee is popular, tea was the drink of choice in this part of the world.

As the women disappeared into the kitchen, I stood on the veranda of this house which seemed to be protruding out of the side of the hill station. Facing the house was another massif with red, yellow, purple, and green houses of different hues sitting slanted along the verges of the sloped margin.

It was a crisp, chilly air. In the mirage, sitting quietly, was the turquoise and white Himalayan landscape. The sunlight bounced off the white iron chairs, similar to the bistro-style seating we have in Canada. The men sat behind me taking in the beauty, eyes staring to the horizon, wandering over the scene.

I decided to accompany the women in the kitchen.

For the first time, I had the experience of watching as coffee was made by stirring the dry grounds with a few drops of water. This turned frothy and then the hot water was poured from a heavy iron pot, stirred some more and then into a gold-plated Prince Albert teacup and saucer.

I still remember the aroma, flavor, and freshness of it.

Tired, I wanted a bath and relaxation. Mina's mother insisted that before that, I must drink milk infused with saffron and turmeric, haldi to preserve my beauty.

She was kind, and I had to respect her wishes, so I did it with hesitation and the knowledge there was no beauty left of me, inside or outside. I was a hollow illusion of splendor.

The afternoon monsoon began abruptly.

The din and friction of thunder and lightning took the electricity out. For the first time in my life, I bathed with water heated by a stove. Two large terra cotta buckets with rounded silver handles were placed in the bathing room, one with cold and the other with hot water.

The bathing room was a large structure of sandstone and limestone, dimly lit but comfortable. In the corner, an iron and silk stool sat quietly with a vanity set. Crisp white towels and a beautiful robe were placed on the chair for me.

Somehow the bath, without the modern touches, was a tender, natural experience. The hum of my hand splashing water provoked a mundane mystery.

I missed my family.

To feel completely immersed and at one with the inhabitants of this newfound heaven in the midst of perdition, I removed my gilded pashmina shawl from my suitcase. I wore it to join the rest in the dining room. Most adults—young, old, male, female—wore a shawl draped over their shoulder, so I did too, desperate to submerse myself with the rest. Regardless of my efforts, I would never be accepted.

I was the foreigner.

With my cloak draped around me, I returned to the drawing room.

There was a relaxed and hushed atmosphere. Perhaps for the first time in my life, I listened more than I spoke.

I knew only a few vagrant words of a dialect completely unknown to me. I listened as the elders decided we must visit Kausani.

Kausani is one of the closest and most beautiful points one may reach toward the Himalayas.

The driver took us through Nainital, Talital, and then Kausani. How ironic I was immersed in this breathtaking scenery, having the worst experience of my life.

I can never forget the revolving bus ride upward to reach the top of the ridge at an altitude of 1,890 meters. The bus drove hurriedly, around and around at the edge of the Someshwar Valley.

Dressing the slant downward was the splendor of opaque emerald pine trees. I felt I could drop over the edge, deep into the vale as I stared down in awe, circling upward.

The guide spoke periodically about temples and marble and stone remnants, idols that had historical or religious significance.

Half empty, the bus carried six couples. I sensed their abrasive bonds, wondering if any of them loved each other. All were taking in the beauty, fresh air, and panoramic scene. We stopped briefly at a tiny hill station for tea, served at the roadside. The outdoor flames were fanning the black copper bottom of the old iron kettle, and in the open air, the smoke swirled in cloudy designs. Behind the tea stall, there was a stream with the clearest water I had ever seen flowing down age-old rocks. We finally reached our destination. If I could ever envision heaven, this would have been the perfect scene.

After tirelessly pleading, I was granted my request to stay alone. In my chalet, loneliness was my company. I spoke with her at length, telling her I was the symbol of perfection, obedience, and self-sacrifice, not in my own eyes, but in the eyes of others.

She understood my soul was destroyed for this.

I was the caged bird who desperately wanted to fly away, to escape the prison of my own tyranny. It was in Kausani that I came to this realization, one that altered the trajectory of my entire life. The silence gave life to the bedrock of my professional and personal life pursuits, ones that became etched in my soul.

In seclusion, I realized the significance of self-mastery. After my return to Canada, my aspiration to research and write on self-mastery came to fruition.

My recollection gave the grave feeling that left everything of those weeks far behind me, never to look back and my remembrance was limited to the feeling that I had lost all self-worth I had ever known, but my tenacity and belief in my Self recaptured my spirit. I decided to research and write about the Self from a scholarly and scientific stance. My only purpose was to share the knowledge we must nurture our self before all else. Only after this can we give the best of who we are to others.

Fall, 2002

Knowledge of Self Begins with Self-Mastery

At the University of Toronto, I successfully conducted research studies on the importance of self-worth and how a strong or weak sense of self can affect education and lifelong success.

I describe self-mastery as moments in time, from nine seconds, nine minutes, nine hours, nine days, nine weeks, nine months, nine years, or nine decades that you spend in solitude with *you* only. Your being contemplates this existence, your likes and dislikes.

Having knowledge of self is not the same as self-mastery. I exemplify this with being a wine connoisseur. Preference of wine with meals or for social relaxation is not the same as having in-depth knowledge about wine and the complex process of choosing the correct wine for a dish. Similarly, being a casual tennis player is not the same as being a professional player. Experts impart a sophisticated level of analysis and action, which ensures a deep,

thoughtful knowledge base of a subject. *Herewith, the subject is you.*

On this journey, I will guide you as you delve deeper into understanding your Self more than you ever thought possible. Today, our busy lives lack a deeper understanding of self. Rather than the pursuit of superficial self-knowledge, we must delve into a more profound understanding of the Self.

Often we believe we are informed about a topic, and it's only when we explore and *analyze it further that we realize how limited our knowledge actually is.* The idea here is to apply this thought to the subject of *your* Self. The deeper you nurture self-mastery, the more you grasp an understanding of your purpose.

During moments of complete self-immersion and self-thought, you advance the talent to recognize who you truly are *and* want to be. These are moments when your being is not dissolved by interaction. It is not affected by the presence, needs, and assumptions of others. (This is especially true for women.) The usage of the word "dissolved" assumes we manage our impressions and dilute the Self during exchanges. We cannot get away from this dissolution. To communicate effectively requires empathy otherwise, we would be acting selfishly. We are never our complete Self until we are alone. Even then, we are subtly affected by society.

Moments of self-mastery are moments in time which we relegate for interacting with our own undecorated, undissolved Self.

War, hate, environmental disregard, human trafficking, child labor and exploitation, abuse, hunger, and civil conflict have not been eradicated despite humanity's advances and technologically placed innovations. Why are we still seeking to quell our problems from without rather than from within? Rather, we must begin first with our self and reach inwardly.

How can we hold *real* compassion for anyone if we do not for our own Self and for those closest to us? Compassion for others is predicated on self-respect. This kind of self-respect is dependent on self-mastery. Thus, there is a synergistic relationship between self-mastery and our treatment of others. How does this occur? I will explain.

The Science of Self-Mastery: An Equation

Throughout my writing, self-mastery is a complex web of personal creations of the Self. It refers to your existence as a manifestation of your feelings of inner self-worth. You master your sense of self-worth during the time spent with *yourself for yourself.* Your worth is generated by you alone. Others can assist you to nurture it, but you are its keeper. Your kindness and the empathy you have towards others is a direct correlation to the sense of self-worth you feel.

The self-mastery equation is:

Greater Self-Mastery = Stronger Self-Worth + Greater Kindness Toward Others

Less Self-Mastery = Weaker Self-Worth + Less Kindness Toward Others

The Self Algorithm

My ideas about self-mastery draw from the various disciplines of sociology, social psychology, biology, philosophy, physics, and neuroscience. I am a social scientist, and my strengths lie thus.

I believe the discipline of sociology is more important in today's world than ever before. Even as the superiority of technology and the Internet connects us digitally, humans, businesses, organizations, and nations cannot flourish without face-to-face interaction with one another. More than ever, we must network, cooperate, and communicate with people of unique cultures, religions, and economic status from our own.

Thus, we require knowledge of the effective modes of interaction for personal and professional success on this universal playground. Recognition of this is upheld by the understanding that beyond every interaction we experience, one element lingers: the way the person makes *you* feel.

Sociological concepts help to guide our interactions and understanding of others' viewpoints. We form and manage the impressions we have of each other because we seek their approval. Above all, we must make the most profound designs of who we are first to draw others in.

We cannot communicate effectively, fairly, and with empathy unless we have a grasp of social affairs, social life, and the concepts that guide our social existence. For this reason, I believe the social assessment set forth is an effective tool for mastery of Self.

Self-mastery is the process and the action required for realizing your self-worth. Envision the question of self-mastery as this: How can I know and be kind to anyone else—my child, lover, parent, friend, family, neighbor, or colleague—if I am not kind to myself or do not know myself first?

Definition: One important dimension of self-mastery is it guides us to overcome our weaknesses. Its practice creates a strong manifestation of our self *for* our self, nobody else. We must have and nurture self-mastery because it lets us think, envision, and drive inner power to effectively negotiate the many dimensions of our existence *beyond* our fears.

Our human purpose is to live life fully, create a better world, be aware, be present and act with intention. Asking questions and drawing universal conclusions is what makes scientific inquiry powerful.

This type of inquiry must extend to our understanding of self. We no longer ask questions, such as: What will be my legacy? Who am I? What is my purpose? What matters most to me? These have been replaced with: Did you get my text? Did you check your email? Will you attend the

meeting? What is the child's schedule? This particular way of thinking has manifested in stress, addictions, obesity, heart disease, mental disorders, and cancers, which remain on the rise.

Environment, diet, exercise, genetics, and many other factors play into the negative forces facing our societies of today. Additionally, we must consider how the broken connection and lack of fluidity between overt action and inner purpose have affected our lives.

Our reality is heavy with action-oriented activities that lie external to the realm of self.

A few years ago, I was at an airport. I sat with my girls, waiting for our flight. Looking around, I discerned a common scene. Everyone had some type of micro-machinery in hand. No one had a book in hand except a well-coiffed hyper-nervous mother in her forties, who was reading to her sleepy toddler. Her baby sat drowsy-eyed on her flowery pink-skirted lap. He was fighting sleep to stay awake so he would not miss all of the bustling activity.

As any well-meaning mother, she seemed to take every opportunity to instill the love of reading. She mumbled words from a vividly colored hardcover book. A small Kindle reader was encased in the book itself and seemed redundant. I suppose she wanted the choice of using the electronic book to comfort her child if he was restless. If that did not work, then having the real thing was an option.

To me, nothing electronic can take the place of the look, feel, smell, touch, and sensation of fingers pondering across paper as one turns the pages of a real book.

To the left of her, in a corner chair, an impatient man about sixty was fiddling with a tarnished silver antique pocket watch in one hand and an iPhone in the other, his head rotating from watch to phone screen. The phone rang in vibration, and he answered in a deep raspy voice.

Four red-fabric chairs down from him, a woman not more than thirty sat seemingly sleepy while looking over her itinerary, laptop in lap with a screensaver that flashed *"Excelsa Petite."* This especially caught my attention, because it's a Latin phrase meaning "strive for that which is greatest."

From that simple line, I thought she was someone I wanted to interact with. Next to her sat two burgundy carry-ons. One with a black-, green-, and white-striped scarf tied on the key chain, the other with a pink scarf tied on its keychain.

Begrudgingly, I wondered what she had in those. With a sense of guilt, I thought how nice it would be to travel so light, no stroller, no baby bags, no thermometer, no medication, no pull-ups, no coloring books, no toys, no snacks, and no carrying three sets of clothes for me and my two little ones—only myself, and the things I loved to have with me during travel.

What would these be? I had almost forgotten. Most probably, a recent issue of an academic or literary journal, my own pretty Chanel scarf of navy and yellow, my favourite Prada or Tory Burch wedge shoes, my comfortable blue and black Mei jeans; blouses and t-shirts in a vast array of colors, a formal-looking skirt and blazer, most likely in navy, definitely Lulu workout tights and tank, and a makeup bag.

Disappointed at my present reality and the thought that such realms of packing my luggage were far out of reach, I sat looking outside through the floor-to-ceiling glass walls. It was just after noon. The sun was brightly yellow.

I saw a bird— a robin.

While a common bird, the likelihood of having time to appreciate its presence was impossible in my busy life.

Suddenly, I had time, forced upon me in waiting for a flight.

I could tell it was a robin from the orange underbelly. She flew, looking lovely against the crisp blue backdrop of the sky. She flew out of my view into the airfield, then into my view again. Somehow, I knew when she flew away, she was meant to return to my view.

I was playing a silent game of pursuit with this bird. She landed gently, sitting on the outstretched wingtip of the grounded plane.

I was amazed at the little flickers of the neck, the side glances and pausing gaze.

I wondered if she was beholding me admiring her.

I envisioned how freeing it would be to fly, to have wings as the robin. In that instant, a moment of intense self-absorption, a moment of self-mastery, I learned considerably about myself. For mere minutes, I was ensconced in thoughts of simply being.

Amid the hundreds of people in this bustling airdrome with the background humming and the symphony of

various plane's engines, I recaptured a childhood love of the robin.

It was a typical springtime bird that flew in our temperate backyard, beckoning the freshness of spring on the horizon, my birthday season.

I would gaze at the backyard through the drawn glass doors speckled with droplets of rain. In utter and pure contentment, I would watch the robin exist. I was awed by the slight glints of her head, oblivious to being seen.

She looked anywhere she wanted, no one to discern. I wanted to be like that bird.

Even at eight years old, I knew.

Lost in this scene, I was taken back to those beautiful moments of my childhood. Sorrowfully, mind wandering, I wondered why these moments were so few. It was freeing, and I felt more connected to myself than I had for a very long time.

There was an unfulfilled emptiness that lingered. I realized I was lacking moments of solitude. The moment I experienced was found *only* because of my wait for a flight.

It was "me" time thrust upon me. It was a quiet solitude found in a place of noise.

These are the finite interactions that make us who we are. Today, alone-filled moments are rare. We do not prioritize personal introspection regularly. Instead, we set "vacation" time for it. If we are to grow and enliven our spirit, and the spirit of others, we must take the time to place our attention inwardly, consistently.

The robin is an extended metaphor of my life and this work. In images of this bird, I have found escape and solace during my most trying times.

In Kausani, the monal, an endemic bird to the Himalayan region, took the place of my friend the robin.

June, 2016

A Tuesday morning, hurried as usual, I recall backing my car out of the driveway to take my girls to school.

The rushing halted.

I observed a mother robin and her baby flying around on the green grass atop our front lawn. The girls were so thrilled to see the mother bird playfully pecking around the grass with her baby. In that moment, everything stopped. I realized my daughters had never seen a baby robin so closely.

I said, "Look at this. It's a sight so rare, I don't care if you're late today."

I put down the windows, and my two girls and I sat for a few minutes watching the mama bird and her baby as they merrily leaped about while bees buzzed around the newly yellow and red blooming tulips in the backdrop.

It was one of the most bonding moments I have had with my children.

My little one said, "Mama, you play with us like the mommy bird."

My darlings were inspired by the beauty of a natural scene. They realized and savored the usual and mundane connection of the mother bird and her offspring. It was an ordinary occurrence, unforeseen, unplanned and sporadic, yet vastly powerful.

The robin is not an exquisite bird like the golden pheasant or bohemian waxwing.

Humbly, she is not regarded as an exotic thing of beauty as other rare birds. Her familiarity is what makes her plain and enticing.

Yet her beauty intrudes with mystery.

Her beguiling qualities are imposed in precisely our acquaintance with her; this is her rare quality.

We take her for granted because she is easily and quietly present during much of the year.

She is simply there.

We think this way of our self. After knowing someone for a very long time, have you ever felt or realized you do not know them at all?

We want to get to know people in order to acquaint ourselves with them, we grow to like them, and they may have an important role in our lives. How often do we get to know our self? Have you ever felt you do not know yourself? In the business of life, we take our self for granted because we are a part of our self.

Rarely do we reconnect with our spirit. We seek familiarity with the more glamourous representations in our life. We seek to know what our favorite personalities are doing, whether it is a singer, artist, actor, celebrity.

We believe their lives are the ideal. They are not.

We seek the ideal to diminutive and destructive ends. While we never think we are capable of skydiving or

mountain climbing, if we try it, it may invigorate us. The feeling could imitate nirvana. We may realize how awesome mountain climbing is, how good it feels. This is how self-mastery operates. The more you seek it out, the more pleasurable and fulfilling it becomes.

The questions we ask are directed to things *outside* the self. Individuals no longer ask questions of intrinsic value. We have become the work ship of our material existence. Often, we are criticized for not setting aside time for family and friends, and rarely do we ask ourselves: *Did I make time for me today?* In fact, if we do, it resonates as egocentric. Most vitally, the personal time we set aside is, in fact, the most important part of our daily sequence.

For example, your neighbor may prioritize seeing a very ill family member; this is her priority and considered the right thing to do.

Thus, after work, your neighbor visits a sick relative in the hospital; she spends the rest of the day completing a host of errands and goes to bed exhausted. Your neighbor and most of us would believe she had a productive day. She used her time to complete important practical errands and spend emotional time with family and people who need her to "be there."

The peril of this type of thinking is it creates a vulnerability, which in turn weakens our spirit and sense of self. Often, we never recognize this danger. Daily fulfillment of goals with practical or emotional ends, the idea of "being there" for others, is merely action oriented and not thoughtfully processed.

Failure to take moments to *contemplate* the various activities that took place in a particular day disregards the *deeper sensibility* of how the interactions affect us. In the neighbor's case, perhaps there is a concern about a prognosis or concern for how the rest of the family are coping with an illness. If she does not take alone time to switch off, and think, she cannot manage those feelings inwardly. She remains treading on front stage.

During times when important decisions are being made, we often ask to "think about it." We want time to "think" so we are confident our decision is the correct one. Often this is done in significant personal, financial, and practical matters of life such as buying a home, getting married, or changing careers.

We falter desperately with this mindset; we leave our thinking to what we define as the most life-altering decisions, when in fact every day of our life defines us.

Thus, we must practice the "think about me" process daily and not for practical ends alone. Using a "think about me" mantra centers us upon "me," and we are not only thinking about "it."

Taking moments for solitude creates a deeper articulation of our experiences and crystallizes important facets of our existence, which *stem from those experiences*.

Our experiences are not actualized fully without an articulating depth and purpose. We are left with a weakened sense of self and feelings of vulnerability if we do not think about our actions and other's actions in relation to our own, on a daily basis. Our experiences

become preserved on a superficial level if we do not give thoughtful expression to them.

How many non-actualized experiences are we all carrying?

To remain on the smooth surface of activities in daily life without deeper consideration of our experiences, we simply remain. We forget the effective strategies of coping and we lose the understanding of why we must exist for our self, nobody else.

The Self Insignia

If we take ten minutes—I realize for many of us, even ten minutes can be difficult to set aside for alone time—we craft an important internal dialogue. The Self button is switched on. Switching on to the self means we are simply not *reacting* to the minute events and interactions of our day. Rather, self-time actualizes our thoughts towards *contemplation* of the various activities. This appraisal is what elicits self-mastery because we think about our own actions *in relation* to other's actions.

The feelings you carry from the day's activities become nuanced. This deeper thinking of our surface-oriented existence is at the heart of self-mastery. It is different from overthinking or ruminating upon a problem. As individuals, we are the controllers of the self-time badge because we hold the power to adjust, dim, and brighten it for optimal success. The point is we must recognize we hold this power.

Often, when family and friends are stressed, we want to give assistance and support. At times, assisting becomes the priority and takes precedence; we ignore other facets of life.

Failure to retreat and consistently giving of our self creates health problems. Eventually, we move so far away from the self that we cannot connect with our own problems. When upset we are told to "forget it," to not "think about it." We attempt to displace the pain rather than own it. While a complex process, this mindset can result in dependency or addictive behavior.

In coping with life matters and the demands placed upon us by those we care for, we retreat by becoming either depressed, anxious, or isolated. I am not suggesting we not support each other; however, we must balance support with loving for the self too.

We may stay tuned in to our stress completely, and this too can lead to disruptive emotional issues and addictions. Women may make time to go on a retreat for serenity. The danger is we think of coping and reconnecting as a special occasion, which is dangerous. We must connect with our Self daily in order to cope effectively.

The everyday—and not the sporadic—practice of self-mastery helps us learn to manage stressful situations. We practice gradual turning on and off as a process and build upon it with the accumulation of self-knowledge. The goal is to accumulate self-mastered knowledge gradually. Without self-mastery, when we are thrown into a whirlwind of uncertainty, or in times of unexpected upheaval, and life

happenings we cannot effectively harness the best of our self, because we have not put effort toward nurturing and understanding it. This does not and cannot occur overnight.

The common phrase of overthinking something is the other extreme whereby we cannot stop our contemplation of an aching problem, real or imaginary. The idea here is to thrive for balance in all things. I do believe that if we fall into the realm of overthinking, this too is a manifestation of a person who lacks self-mastery.

Overthinking, anxiety, rumination can be side effects of psychological, emotional, abusive trauma and can worsen with a lack of connection to self. Feeling anxious leads us to self-isolate, and this also creates a vicious cycle.

Currently, in the midst of modern existence, atrocities of war and hate are rampant. Why does suffering persist? If we do not know and nurture our own being, how can we expect to be capable of nurturing the well-being of others close to home and afar? Do we require a new way of thinking? Rather, should we be looking from within ourselves and not from without?

Leaving the Self switched on with only small doses of time for self-mastery affects our lives negatively, as I have tried to demonstrate. If practiced with everyday consistency through the stages of life, self-mastery enables effective strategies for coping, from childhood to adolescence, to young adulthood, the mid-years and beyond.

In the next chapter, I share my experiences and intellectual knowledge of how selfishness begets selflessness.

Chapter Two, Summary: Chapter two begins with a prolonged metaphor comparing the incongruent similarities of life and death. My opening poetry here, idealizes humanity's quest of seeking forever youth. We must not disrespect the process of aging as we move toward death from life. Beauty lies in the wisdom begotten of aging, lest we forget this in our youthful pride. I then discuss how selfishness breeds selflessness.

The Paradox of Selfishness

So familiar yet so strange is the dissonance of life. A paradox is a contradiction, opposites that coexist at the same time. In life and death, we find humanity's greatest paradox. It is an enigma, rationalized with merciless persistence. Yet if we search deeply, there is an element of logic warped in absurdity. The contradiction of life and death are puzzling; inevitably, one gives way to the other in the endless cycle of nature.

I illustrate here what I refer to with the paradox of selfishness and why it is the nucleus of self-mastery. Today selfishness is stigmatized, and we must rethink how we look upon what it is to be selfish.

My premise is that selfishness breeds selflessness, and herein is the paradox for the practice of self-mastery. I have drawn on an extended metaphor of life and death, the greatest paradox of all. I have taken my own understanding of youthful yet naive beauty found in early life and contrasted it to the wrinkled presence of the aged. Wisdom is at once played to the hands of the aged, while leaving forlorn youth far behind. We are flawed to think that wisdom is wasted on the old and fragile, while youthful glory is cloaked in the wondrous beauty of naïveté.

We must value the wisdom of the aged as we stand in arrogance with youthful beauty.

Life and Death: An Extended Metaphor of Life's Greatest Paradox

Her straight hair, thinly plaited with but three hundred strands. It is a preservation of fallen beauty from a full dancing mane.

Never to see the waning in the distance, drop by drop, the blackish brown tresses softly transform to a coiled silvery torrent.

The tragedy lies in a forgotten remembrance of the fertile days of youth.

Fluttering, spirits afloat in the wind of gratification, thinking imaginary and beautiful thoughts.

Elapse in time.

A realization, blurred not to be seen. The past, present, and future become pigmented in plain sight. A colored solitude turns to debauched disarray. Passage of time, *tempus fugit*, fizzles. Destined by death's eternal momentum,

There lies a disarray of blankness, a looming void of nothingness.

She sits in her tarnished copper armchair. Blanketed, her back rubs the flattened cushion, morose from overuse.

Unable to recollect for even a fleeting moment, she searches for a bemused blunder of demented delight.

Destiny calls.

The seconds contradict the minutes that condemn the hours. Cracked are the days as they foil into a motif of a mundane annual ascent in transience. The moratorium transforms into a pensive permanence.

The stench of the aged misery, despair not, for you too shall meet her. She permanently affixes her gentle ghost upon the horizon for all to embrace. Not ever to vanish and always vehemently victorious.

Youthful arrogance, your fate in destitution.

We shall quiver at her disappearance, it supposes an impossible immortality. The evaporation transforms from a luminous sultry place. An undesirable presence supervenes.

A dialectical disturbance created by youth yearning to stay in an old bundle.

Alas, the capsule cloaked in a shoe, keys to cut the fruit, an apple. The reckoning of an ancient school day, the boy whispers.

"I like you." she tells me with a smile.

"It happened today when we rolled down the green hill of grass," she continues, about the vacation she had seven decades ago, but is happily packing for when I ask, "Where are you going?"

She speaks and scolds his framed image for being late for dinner.

Again.

The knife becomes the narrow comfort of steel in the bosom, nebulous of pain. Dispensed is a permanence of waiting, in a room of smoky haze. In a soundless silence of abuse, suffering creeps, as tears of dewdrops fall.

Melting away, the moments become muffled.

A sparse solace collected in synaptic streaks of a cherished childhood calls.

The intellect ridicules and larks.

Fading.

To enchanted chaos she moves, floating aimlessly toward the waif of wailing. The soul assembles itself, sorrowfully with indolence. The languor lingers far after the brain resolves not to play.

He shuts you out selfishly.

Emotion is mocking the body as it sits *alive in death*.

Outstretched, the wrinkled arms call, trapped in an infirmary of ambivalence. The only predetermination in the chaos of existence is that birth will embrace death.

They become one, only to separate as one.

The atom forms a vapor of sublimation, as the machine slows.

Its permanence is the fluidity of passages far away.

The veins become grains, melting by the death of gravity.

The muse is the molecular ocean of matter. In her depths the somber stones descend.

Nobody watches.

Only the quietly sobbing armchair, punctured with holes in its discolored fabric.

Hollow and heavy holes of dignity expose a vainglory pride turned to resignation.

Humiliation is concealed in the vanity of the aged disdainfully. Insolent aging leaves her tyrannical torture for all to touch.

Fortune smiles upon the preserved youth of the chosen that death embraces early. They are her darlings—the jewels that gleefully sparkle, devoid of the indignant walk toward the horizon.

This was her story.

Eyes empty and bereft of will, neither pleasure nor purpose found. Lost in an auric daze, the masses of life's passage become bricks of mortar, drowning in her shadow of pestilence.

A burial for the barrier between life and death, it is a thin golden thread that bonds her and the passing. A pendulum swayed in a blanket of nothingness. Both have forsaken her in the midst of longing.

How can it be that life and death are devoid of permanence?

Life is fought in unfairness whilst death deduces us to desolation. Moments of fleeting, happiness must hasten, so that misery may meander itself upon us; taunting us for seconds, rarely for days. Less erratic is the lasting of contentment for it arrives and leaves before it is even known.

Decades lost quickly, as we delight in a momentary affront.

Titillated by its presence, existence leaves us suddenly as we yearn for more.

The Enigma of Selfhood

A paradox exists: You must be selfish to accomplish the goal of self-mastery so that you may feel a strong sense of self-worth. At the onset of this work, I was torn.

How shall I convey to my readers that we need to be selfish to be happy and emotionally fulfilled? I knew I truly felt this; more importantly, I believed it. In retrospect, the decision to write about this topic was made early on. I needed that mindset to act upon it. I shared the initial experience for the paradox with you in the first chapter.

My unselfish acts created deep voids that brought me to the realization that, to be happy and your best for others, you must begin with yourself.

Everyone could in some way relate to my message. How? My ideas about life are clear: The way we exist, interact, and treat one another affects how we come to think of ourselves. *Our interactions are not only about the way we make others feel, but they are also about the way we make ourselves feel.*

This is a principle that we can all relate to, regardless of race, class, culture, ethnicity, educational level, sexual orientation, ability, or religion. From birth and beyond, we are taught that to feel worthy, we must give love unconditionally and we must help others, and self-sacrifice is a moral imperative. It is not. This mode of thinking is, in fact, what limits us from our self.

In our world, selfishness is regarded with stigma. *We all want to feel good about our self, and we are led to believe the only way to reach this goal is by making sacrifices, to put our needs aside and be helpful for the sake of others.* Our ability to do so is limited by our assumptions of self-perception (I am a good singer, but I cannot draw or paint). Surely we have endless capabilities to be our best and feel good without another person's input. Yet we tend to frame everything we do from the standpoint of wanting to make others' lives better. With this, we ceaselessly seek *their* legitimation of our self.

Is it wrong to believe that, for example, you volunteer to feel fulfilled about you *first,* to think you are composed to help others, once you have a healthy sense of your own self-worth?

Modernity has taught us to be the best, pursue our dreams, and the fruits of our achievements are because of our own actions. For success to happen, we must be self-absorbed. Yet, we shy away from admitting that it is a necessary part of our existence. Being self-contained is what moves us to succeed to greater heights and in doing so, we are better situated to help others to do the same.

Self-mastery requires self-seeking. You prepare yourself to be in control of you. With control, you see things from other standpoints. This action not only empowers you, but it empowers others. Hence, *mastery of you* is the talent of knowing who *you* are so that you *can* understand others and interact empathetically.

The process is evolving and not linear. We experience elevated self-confidence at certain points in our lives where self-mastery is heightened. Other times, we lack self-assurance in moments of adversity where our potential for self-mastery may have waivered.

As humans, we are equal in our ability to practice self-mastery, our circumstances, genetics and experiences vary, but we all have the potential to exercise it. Self-mastery does not require money, power, status, resources, or networking. All we need is our sentient being and aloneness, contemplation.

Today, our mindset is that solitude has a price tag; for example, taking time out for "you" is no longer a priority—why should it be? We often choose to spend leisure time in pursuit of activities that nurture a hobby predicated on social status, or we decide to help a friend, update our social media status, or attend an event. Do not misunderstand me, I do not infer we should not participate in activities, but balance is the key. The inescapable impression is that time spent in solitude is wasted because we *assume* we are placing relationships, duties, roles, and work as secondary.

Time alone is often thought to be "selfish." In today's world, we hesitate to seek seclusion away from our family, friends, devices, and computers, even for a moment.

This is the path to self-destruction.

The deeper we self-master, the wider we can cast our net of compassion and kindness. At the most basic level, self-mastery gives rise to dignity. The further self-mastery is practiced, the more one can aptly feel a natural compassion for others, a compassion that becomes second nature and never derived.

Possession of a strong inner self creates in us a natural ability to exude an acceptance for others. Indeed, we must always give consideration to individual, personality, biological, psychological, and physiological factors in our ability to do this.

In general terms, acceptance of individual variances is the most positive aspect of self-mastery. How does this occur? As with any talent, the practice of the basic skills fortifies the talent. We challenge ourselves further to the next level. Similarly, while self-mastery is about *you,* when you practice it with dedication, you are better poised to appreciate yourself at a deeper level. This appreciation extends to others.

Self-mastery creates awareness of you, and you connect yourself to the rest of the world. This promotes harmony and consideration toward others. When I think of generosity, persons of distinction such as Oprah Winfrey, Bill and Melinda Gates, and Ellen DeGeneres, among others, come to mind for their awareness and generosity to help those in need.

To reach their position, hard work and attention to the needs of their own self *is* required and continues onward. Success in their respective vocation requires they give personal attention to their goals. With their success, they have become symbols of compassion. Self-mastery allows kindness to flow. To understand you builds confidence, it creates an opening to understand others.

Children and Self-Mastery

The practical effects of self-mastery can be observed everywhere. For instance, at the park, you may see children who initially struggled with mastering the skill of playing soccer. The child who resists but keeps working at developing his skills becomes a better player, over time.

Steadily he practices and improves the skill set. Later, he teaches and assists his peers to build their skills for playing soccer or any sport. What is notable is that initially the child *was* self-absorbed in trying to build his own skills. The confidence derived when the talent is mastered in turn motivated the child to help peers. This is where self-mastery takes us.

By deriving strength from those self-absorbed instances, we prepare ourselves to have the consideration of *wanting* to help others. This is not an imposed kindness, it is one that stems from the heart. It flows naturally. This style of kindness is missing in the world today and could perhaps help to explain why conflict and civil rivalry persist, and why competition in the workplace is often hostile.

Treating each other compassionately within our borders and across the globe has become an anomaly due to the pervasive disregard for another's suffering or comportment. Could this be an effect of a world lacking practices of self-mastery?

Thus, self-mastery at a deeper level opens our minds and hearts. Essentially, it leads us to the acceptance of people from races, cultures, and classes unique from our own, both within and without our society.

Eventually, your understanding of you enhances your appreciation of the others' plights. In turn, you can utilize your self-mastered skills for guidance toward altering harmful worldviews regarding humanity. For example, a child growing up in a disruptive home environment may bear witness to disagreements between his parents. He overhears offensive remarks made to his mother, insults about a "woman's place." The same child, when engrossed in the solitude that opens the doors to self-mastery, could independently create thoughtful meanings from what he has heard.

He deals with it.

A deeply disturbed child would obviously require other interventions, but generally speaking, although immersed in a home environment that diminished the existence of women, moments of self-mastery would allow the same child to contemplate and think about what is right or wrong for *him*, rather than what was imposed in the home.

As an adult, this child may become a champion for women's equality, an interest that would have arisen from deep contemplation about his mother's position in society, despite having heard negative messages. Herein lies the power of solitary moments.

It is the responsibility of parents to instill this mode of action alongside daily activities. The lack of time for self-

mastery could have lasting and lifelong consequences. It is notable here that children are unique and outcomes can depend on a myriad of genetic and environmental factors too.

Regardless of position, power, influence, being a child or adult, with the self-given privilege of freedom, self-mastery enhances the potential to make informed decisions for ourselves. You may ponder how a child can do this? Today, children are not always given opportunities for enhanced solitude because there are many distractions undermining the practice.

Because self-mastery allows *you* to articulate *your* own ideas about life, undisturbed and in solitude, the result is a better foundation for coping with your troubles. Solitude is important for creating effective interactions in the immediate social environment, and children need to be provided with opportunities to do so.

From over-scheduling activities to social media, children have been conditioned to equate solitude to boredom. In fact, the pervasive fallacy is that children who prefer being alone are "social misfits." We stigmatize children labeled as the "loner" or who play unaccompanied. When observing a playground, parents are left wondering about the child who is not interacting with the rest or does not participate in extracurricular activities.

We place the social butterflies on a pedestal, and while children need this type of social connection for success, the balance of social activities with solitude is important. Children and adults who choose the less collective pathway should not pay the price of being stigmatized. Susan Cain brings our awareness to the power of introverts.[i]

This is not to say we cannot make decisions with others. As a social scientist, I recognize our interactions are paramount to an ardently healthy life. However, self-mastery elevates interactions to *unfold more effectively.*

The Self-Mastery Skill Set

In the corporate world, most decision-making derives from teamwork. Effective leaders will permit team members to give independence of thought toward decisions. Moreover, good leaders are aptly able to understand a colleague's stance, even if nuanced differently from their own.

Team leaders become effective by having an elevated sense of their self-worth. Further, self-mastery enables leaders to be practitioners of compassion in the corporate world. A leader who listens to diverse opinions and does not feel threatened if her power is challenged retains a strong sense of self, which is ultimately guided by self-mastery.

The leader's power is used to mobilize the best in others. This is the effective influence that is the engine of positive leadership in the corporate world, an attribute that people in their personal and professional lives require. Failure to act with understanding toward colleagues and acquaintances stimulates a tense environment.

Arrogance is the mode by which individuals hope to attain power and respect. The focus is on *their own self* first

during interactions, and the message communicated is "I matter more." Self-mastery replaces arrogance with unassuming empathy. How does this occur in the working world?

Self-importance, steeped from arrogance, creates and impresses upon the other that *I*, the leader, am more important, rather than equal to *you*, the follower. While there is an imbalance depending on roles or titles, we are equal on a human level, and we must begin at this point for effective interactions to occur.

Time that is spent with the Self profoundly nurtures our capacity to genuinely understand other people's viewpoints, even if they are different from own.

Thus, interactions occur with a fluidity that imparts a message to others of "Yes, your ideas do matter, even if they are unique from my own."

This is a thought process that extends to various types of relationships.

"Selfish moments" are the ones that give rise to connecting with those we value personally and professionally. For example, when in a heated argument with a colleague or a partner, are we *really* able to understand their viewpoint? It is only when we "cool off," spending time in solitude, that we realize the person had a valid stance, or not. Self-mastery nurtures the tools to understand these momentary affronts.

Ironically, when you spend time alone, you can understand others' perspectives because in practicing self-mastery, you have cultivated an understanding of your own

viewpoints first. This opens the door for acceptance of unique views. You gain a better understanding of contradictions, inconsistencies between you and others.

The most powerful effect of self-mastery is that you retain your *own* self-worth and treat others in a way that retains *their* self-worth.

Self-Mastery Leads to Personal Success

How often are you faced with the dilemma of having to learn new skills? On a daily basis in our ever-transforming information age, we are confronted with having to acquire a new skill, whether it is a basic computer program or starting a new job. If I asked you to list ten skills you have mastery of, what would they be? Take a moment and list these before reading on.

Would you contend that the mastery of your self is one of your ten greatest skills?

The mastery of you does not happen unless you exert energy toward it. The individual maintains numerous choices as to what should be done with their free time. You may decide to help a friend move house, visit an ailing parent, meet an aunt you have not seen for a long time, or play golf with a colleague, which may help to move your career forward.

Certainly, it is understandable why we would choose activities for goal attainment and socializing, instead of solitude. Fortunately, we live in a society where we are free to choose. Hence, it is a choice to take moments of solitude for the mastery of you. These moments are only created by

you. Whether you decide to make this time for connecting with yourself is in your power.

Diligence and perseverance are required because we can easily become distracted and steer away from the mundane idea of solitude, but it is profoundly the most important part of our day, our purpose, and our life.

A recent study shows that conscientiousness is one of the greatest predictors of success.[ii] If we cannot be conscientious to understanding our own self, how can we become diligent in the pursuit of any talent, or still want the best for others? *Hence, we must be conscientious to practice self-mastery so that we attain the ability to persevere in the pursuit of our goals.*

Therefore, self-mastery *determines* the extent to which we further develop those personality traits required for success. And, while personality traits have a genetic predisposition, we know environmental factors are significant too. Studies have shown the dynamic relationship between nature and nurture factors for character development and personality.[iii]

Here is where we gain control to establish the necessary routines for success. In other words, all qualities required for success must be predicated upon self-mastery. Self-mastery is the bedrock, the foundation, for which all other traits for success flows—*it is the soil in which we plant the seeds of our success.*

Self-mastery is the soil—contentiousness, perseverance, and determination are its flowers that grow.

The flowers cannot grow unless the soil is healthy.

It is during self-mastery that we harvest determination and dedication, traits required for generating growth. We continue to want to work toward our goals.

For example, you may be scheduled to conduct a seminar to demonstrate a campaign for your corporate or professional team. You feel there is a setback because the seminar did not flow as you wanted.

If you practice articulating the scenario deeply in solitude, you gain a better grasp of the nuances that were played out. You understand how to better foster your talents, rather than fixate on disenchantment. However, if you do not contemplate the situation in solitude, it festers, it becomes unresolved when pushed aside rather than confronted.

We cannot be confined to a superficial understanding of our experiences, regardless of how strong or subtle they may be. If we do not take quiet moments to focus on the good and bad attributes of the day, we mentally and emotionally limit our development. We must think about our own needs, wants, ideas, and desires in relation to our daily experiences. Think of this as a surfer only glides on a wave, failure to delve deeper verdures our actions to remain on the mere surface without moments of self-mastery. Consistency is required in the daily practice of self-mastery. Think of self-mastery as exercise for self, soul,

and spirit, in addition to physical exercise you do for your body, or mental exercise you do for your mind. We cannot ignore our bodies and do all physical activities in a given day; we must be consistent. Similarly, consistency is required for self-mastery.

To consciously and thoughtfully connect from within yourself, you rightfully become self-absorbed. You simply cannot attain this in the company of others. Recalling my extended airport metaphor above, while I was in a busy environment, I was alone because I was not interrelating with anyone, alone time can be found with or without the companionship of others. For example, how does it happen that we can be in relationships for decades and still feel alone?

It is important to note here that alone or in the company of others, society subtly or palpably acts upon us in many ways. In other words, even alone, we are pressed to conform to certain standards, culturally placed values, and norms of our society, and self-mastery brings our conscious awareness to this.

Your Personal Self Manual

We spend our lifetime attaining different skill sets. By the time we acquire the skills toward mastery of a talent, something newer and better takes its place, and the cycle continues. We take time to read manuals, guidelines, commands, rules of how to use our computers, electronic devices, televisions, microwave, multimedia players,

appliances, cars, maps, cookbooks, children's toys and many other "how to" compositions.

Additionally, trying to remain updated in our respective professions and the corporate world has led to over-credentialing. We seek cutting edge skills to retain an advantage over the competition.

Thus, self-improvement for practical skills is beneficial since it impacts our quality of life. Moreover, imagine if we took a fraction of this time and spent even a few minutes per day to master *our* self to create our own personal self-manual for improving.

Limitation of time is one of modernity's greatest challenges. Despite the conveniences we enjoy, even our young children have packed daily schedules. On a human level, is it practical to continue on the path of attaining skills outside of our self, ignoring the most important skill of self-mastery?

Contemplate the effects of not practicing self-mastery, we are continually rotating on a wheel being granted any overt skill but inner self-thought. Our attention is expended on personal relations, work, friendships, placing our own relationship with the self, last.

Selfishness Begets Selflessness: This Is the Paradox of Selfishness

In acting to enrich the lives of others and help family, colleagues, and friends, we are actually acting with self-interest. How? We want and need to feel good about our self.

Extending kindness to others creates fulfillment to feel compassion for others. Yet it is also laden with self-interest. Others may feel gratitude for your help, perhaps they even feel you selflessly helped them, when in fact you acted on the desire to make yourself feel worthy. How is this selfish? I will explain.

For example, you may choose to take care of a sick friend in need. You decide to take a day off work, cook a meal, and be there for your friend. As selfless as your actions may seem, they stemmed from the selfish want to feel good about yourself. Your act translates to and comes across as selfless, but your ultimate goal in the process was to make yourself feel good, and of course also to be helpful. This is one of the most admirable qualities of our humanity.

Some will argue that indeed we can act selflessly and complete selflessness finds its place in pure altruism. A mother's bond with her child is perhaps the clearest example of altruism. She unconditionally, loves, and adores her child, placing everything secondary. I too, believed this prior to becoming a mother. I soon realized it was senseless to deprive myself of sleep, alone-time, different relationships for my children. I realized by ensuring my child sleeps early, I can find time to enjoy the things I once found pleasure in. Indeed, I was acting selfishly, for my own well-being. This is the paradox. Yet we fail to acknowledge and confront the task of the importance of being selfish. Human societies have always advanced by placing the self-first. The social-Darwinian stance is that in order to survive we must elucidate self-centered interests. For our evolutionary progress is dictated by those of us who are best prepared, by placing self-first, we will thrive, survive, have longevity and pass along our genes. We are the "fittest."

Self-mastery is about preserving self-interest, but this is not a selfish interest as I describe above. I refer to this as survival of the masterfully [sic] fittest. At the heart of self-mastery is the ideology that selfishness must occur for personal progress, and this naturally extends to others in the form of empathy.

The Empathy Sequence

Empathetic *describes* how the action should be. I elaborate on empathetic understanding by describing a process that is the guide for a successful life and positive relationships.

Simply having empathy is not sufficient. Many of us have abilities we do not utilize. To act with empathetic understanding is an *intentional process,* imbued with affective action, even assertion. Can we act unconsciously with empathy? Love and affection exist between animals and their offspring, and in humankind. It is existentially nuanced.

Empathetic understanding is a fluid framework that acts as a border to frame our action. Think of a beautiful piece of art, the frame must match or encompass the work effectively. Empathetic understanding thus, varies depending on the situation and interaction. It must enact complementarity.

Unrelenting selfish nurturance of the inner spirit promotes empathetic awareness. It is the most effective building block for self-mastery, this being a practice of selfishness that does not harm anyone. In fact selfishness builds empathy and gives way to stronger interactions. Injury to spirit manifests if we do not practice self-mastery because we ignore the Self, and this ignorance reduces our capacity for empathy.

Failure to feel our best and nurture our own self-worth means we *are* being selfish, because then we do not give our best self to those we care for. Herein we find another paradox of selfishness. The selfishness lies in the point that we are not giving our best self to others. We must be present, accepting and purposeful to nurture the Self independent of others. Once we take the lead, and responsibility, others will help us to thrive too. Think of this as a parent raising a child. The parent gives all of the important necessities, other caregivers, family, community members may help but it is still the primary responsibility of the parent. Similarly, you are the primary caregiver of your Self. Our most finite interactions build toward the formation of self-mastery. Determinate and kind action drives our connections, and in turn creates greater progress in our development of self. Our small and large acts affect us and reinforce self-mastery.

Self-mastery is not refined through material possessions; friends, fans, popularity; it is not distinguished

by power or profession. Individuals can own many possessions yet feel unfulfilled as a lost sailboat floating at sea. Rather, self-mastery advances by the nuances that shape kindness, forgiveness and empathy; these are the actions derived inwardly for the Self and outwardly toward others. This is a purposive two-way dynamic.

A person's existence is valued only through how much they have touched the lives of those they care for. But there must exist at the onset a selfish provocation for helping others. This is the root of self-mastery.

Erving Goffman, renowned sociologist, believed we are actors using "impression management" to communicate and send symbolic cues to each other.[iv] We adopt and prepare for acting in the outside world through the dramaturgical method. Goffman suggests we are all actors enacting roles we perform continuously. We prepare ourselves for our daily performances in the backstage. Props, grooming, self-talk, those things we do not want people to see, often termed as "private" moments. We then act on front stage, performing our rehearsed roles with others. The backstage preparation creates a polished front stage performance. We *act* with confidence and integrity on front stage only when we prepare in the backstage of life. Self-mastery is this backstage preparation.

Moreover, authentic actions regarding the Self take place in the backstage: For example, when getting ready for a meeting, we practice our actions to see how we look, our facial expressions. We speak to ourselves while looking into a mirror. We do this to ensure that our front stage performance is cultured. Most importantly, we act and speak in a way that we *think* the other person will perceive us to be. The process of self-mastery is similarly enacted. Nurturing the self in solitude (backstage) enables a deep concentration of our fears. We interact with the weaknesses that may impede our need to impress and be accepted on the front stage. Through the cycle of engagement with the Self, we gain a better perspective of *why* we should act a certain way on the front stage, and we are not merely acting out of fear or rejection. This self-led engagement leads us to pay attention to our fears rather than push them aside. Our interactions are taken to a superior level, because our knowledge of self is elevated, so that we can give others greater attention. Otherwise we do not interact with confidence. Instead, we may worry or become fearful, even avoid certain people and situations. Such avoidance is not a reflection of the other. In fact it is a reflection of a broken spirit or display a lack of self-mastery. We feel unprepared and self-mastery is that preparation.

The Virtue of "Alone Time"

Aloneness enables an indirect engagement with the opposition we receive from people and situations that trouble us and make us fearful. Solitude creates a forum to challenge our fears. Only when we contemplate our self-doubts can we resolve to devise the actions needed to confront them. Contemplation of what we fear occurs during quiet moments of self-mastery. Today, the value of deep self-importance is undermined and replaced with its shallower version of acceptance by others from afar; for example, the quantity of "friends" or "likes" on social media.

It is perceived as selfish and unkind to seek out time in the day for "you." Even in solace, behind our computers, on our smartphone, we spend free time situating ourselves for others to see, like, accept. The others' opinions have come to take precedence over the opinions we have of our own existence. The more responsiveness, the better one feels in the public forum. We lament upon this endlessly, taking away the reality we must first seek to like our own self *first*. In our moments of self-mastering solace, we pay homage to contradictions that cause inner conflict; for example, if we do not get the attention we appeal for, it does not mean we are flawed.

Articulation of Fear

Fear is our most powerful emotion because fear stems from the mystery and intrigue that surrounds phenomena, place person, or thing that we do not know or have a familiarity of. Knowing alleviates our fears. Knowing yourself alleviates the mystery of your reactions. Knowing how we will react in a social situation and how we will feel allows us to keep our emotions in check. If we have a strong sense of self, and are knowledgeable and aware of how we feel, then we have control of such emotions; most importantly, we know our triggers. Emotional intelligence arises from not repressing emotions, but rather from being

aware of *the type of emotions certain situations would arise in us*.

Self-mastery binds creative contemplation with action. We own our thoughts completely and fearlessly. Fear is our most powerful emotion. Fear exists because of intrigue and mystery of the unknown. Fear guides the intensity by which we feel all other emotions: fear of loss, fear of not being loved, fear of dying, fear of not coping, fear of loneliness, fear of a broken heart, fear of pain. Fear of fear. Backstage performance prepares us for coping with and confronting fear, it is in this place that self-mastery is awakened.

Hence, the arising state is the commitment we make to nurture our self. The manifestation is the positive *ways* in which we can interact with others on the front stage.

Think of all that makes you feel worthy. Then think of what elicits your fears. In the backstage, you articulate and interact with these reservations. With backstage practice, we gain the ability to be more effective on the front stage. *We teach our self to transcend our fears. We gain the penchant for articulating and moving beyond uncertainties. While we may not eradicate fears, we come to an understanding of the underlying sapience of why we fear certain people and situations.* Thus, while we constantly look outside our self for comfort, we often fail to take the most obvious action of looking internally when faced with hardships. In other words, it becomes more difficult to practice the art of self-mastery.

Experts that help us through our problems include therapists, social workers, counselors, medical professionals, and so on, and we must be grateful for dedicated, professional avenues of help with the pressures of life. We must recognize that *alongside* the interventions, we need also to speak and communicate with our self at a deeper level.

The Infinite Front Stage Performance: Why Selflessness is Selfish

Given our busy schedules, professional obligations, and capitalistic competition, it can be argued that individuals today are acting on the front stage constantly. To be relentlessly invested on front stage leaves no room for Self-time.

Complete immersion of Self which favours the front stage dimension of life can have negative consequences. Having become accustomed to being tuned in to the front stage could mean certain individuals experience difficulty in reverting to backstage.

When this happens, we persistently seek self-worth from others. Their personal and professional appraisal of us becomes more important than what we think of ourselves. Thus, self-serving solitude is broken down. Our busy lives and schedules cannot offer us self-worth. The tuned-in-to-front-stage scenario only mystifies and generates a false sense of worth. Today in the whirlwind of technology, Internet, and social media, adults and children are not taking solitude for preparing the self for a healthy front stage performance.

Rather, our necessity to nurture our self remains turned off, and we eventually tune out. The result is a waning sense of self-worth. It can be argued that remaining on front stage for most of our days fuels drug dependency, isolation, and destitution despite the surface ideals of fulfillment.

Can the lack of time we are spending on our backstage life in the quest for dramatizing our self on front stage have negative effects? While we have been taught to believe that knowledge and actions are derived from the outside, and much of it is, self-mastery happens in both the backstage and front stage. The point is to strive for stability. We do not want to remain overly dependent on either the front or backstage of our life performances. Both add value to our overall existence, so we must aim for balance.

Another dimension of the paradox of selfishness is we manage impressions we give others. This can be selfish too, because we want others to feel welcome and comfortable in our presence even if we are uncomfortable. Here I imply that as humans we are programmed naturally by socialization to be kind to each other. In other words, we may act a certain way even if we feel discomfort to make others feel good.

The front stage is not necessarily a manifestation of the authentic self. For example, you may be the host of a party, and a guest arrives with a date who is your ex-partner. You must be pleasant, otherwise you create an unwelcome setting if you are abrasive. As a host, you want to be hospitable to the guests, even if you are upset. In doing so, you want everyone to feel relaxed, but you also want to make yourself look good. You manage your impression for you, and once it feels right for you, it is released to others. This is how selfishness begets selflessness.

April, 2010
The Strong Self

As a first-time inexperienced young mother, I faltered as many well-meaning mothers do. I gave self-sacrificing attention and dedication to my babies from birth to kindergarten. I had no support because we lived four hours away from the rest of our families. I felt I could do everything on my own.

It took six years for me to finally give up. One bright afternoon, depression overcame me. Standing alone on the balcony of my home, looking at the beauty of life in front of me, I could not understand the prevailing hollowness I felt. There was no reason for it.

My daughter played quietly inside. She soon recognized I was not with her and came outside.

"Mama, what are you doing?" she asked.

"Nothing," I answered.

"Mama, do you want alone time?"

At that moment, I realized what she said is powerful. After years of dedicating myself to my roles as mother and wife, and before that as a meticulous student and dedicated family member, I reached the end of this rope—I was yearning and desperately looking to reconnect with *me*.

In giving completely in life, I had lost my sense of self again. I was not even secondary; I became nonexistent, and the most awful part is I *thought* I was doing this for the good of my children. I had separated so far away from myself that I was asking my child to let me be alone, so that I might reconnect with me. Without even realizing what I was implying by my answer, my daughter recognized it in her question.

I wanted to be present and think about me, think about my needs, what makes me who I am. I had forgotten the person, scholar, woman I was. I had forgotten me. I yearned to nurture my own self. In the absence of me, my own self could longer hide its dismay. This became obvious. We cannot give to others fully, unless we give to ourselves *first*. Particularly for women, I have heard many expressions of sacrifice and the negative effects of the constancy of giving on our own self-worth, yet we rarely take action for our own sake.

The nurturance of self-worth builds inner strength. This was a lesson I learned and one that all of humanity must practice. To spend time alone, one becomes a happier, healthier being. When I redirected myself to me, I became a more vibrant and effective being in the lives of those I care for. Are they deserving of anything less? I *knew* this. But the resounding question is why I did not address it—why did it fester for so long, leaving me detached from me?

I waited until I no longer knew me, until my days were lived completely in the dawn. My joys were overtaken with sorrow of the painful detachment. To connect with *me,* regain a mastery of myself *for* myself was the only possibility for me to regain my emotional health. It did not have to be this way, and herein lies my message: Be true to you—it is self-betrayal to ignore your own needs.

The important point is I wanted this not for my children, not for anyone, but for me. This reality set the precedence for my selfish undertaking of the mastery of me. And, in it, I thrived. I felt restored and stronger. Most significantly, I realized something powerful. *Not taking time for solitude, which moved me toward self-mastery, was actually selfish.* How? If we fail to practice self-mastery, we fail to give our best self to our loved ones, and this is selfish. While seemingly paradoxical, I realized my family deserved a mother and wife that took care of herself so she could perform her life roles in the best way possible.

Do your loved ones deserve anything less? In doing so, I am living a life filled with empathy and balance, one that does not forget my needs.

Attaining a mastery of your strengths *first* allows other relationships to flourish with ease. Our society must generate a forum that gives serious consideration to and values the inner self. This is especially true for women and men who are the main caregivers of their children and must balance various obligations.

Thoughtfulness

Selflessness creates a want for the recognition we hope to receive when we espouse energy for others. And perhaps, if recognition is not returned, the "selfless" person eventually becomes disenchanted, causing feelings of dismay. Self-mastery allows us to act without expectation. We do not need the legitimation of others, we *can* legitimate our self, regardless of their action. Whether others return our kindness is not the reason we give it in the first place.

As discussed we act with kindness because we are empathically aware. Performing deeds for others, knowing we are affecting them positively while seeming selfless, *is driven by self-interest* because we feel positive about our self. Our self-interest is utilized to help others; for instance, the act of donating is a wonderfully generous act. In turn, we feel good about our self. This action is based on who we are and channels our attention to our self rather than to the action *itself*. While perceived as selfless, the act of donating is actually selfish because we create a platform for our self to have the sensational feeling of generosity. *This is powerful because this selfish motivation results in holding other people's interests close to our heart.* We act in their interest for our *own* feelings of accomplishment. This is what happens when we practice self-mastery.

It would be deceiving to say human action is without selfish interests. The selfless ideology is altruistic and utopian, I believe far from reach. It is but human nature to act with purpose to protect our self and those we love, we have evolved to survive in this way. However, this deep-seated self-interest is the apparatus, the machinery of compassion. How? To be considerate, there is a prerequisite the self must aspire to. Your self must *want* to

be kind and help others. Simply *showing* thoughtfulness does not imply the *want* to be thoughtful.

Our society has turned interests upside down, deducing the message that we need to be unselfish and non-egocentric. However, for happiness and fulfillment, we need to attend to our interests before turning our attention to others. Success does not imply self-mastery. Many successful persons, though they act with sincere and thoughtful intention, may do so aimlessly out of expectations thrust upon them from the public realm. There is an implied obligation; simply for being successful, individuals are imbued with power. The prosperity, power, and status of celebrities escalate the expectation they should be the keepers of morality. This undue expectation only widens the potential for opening a tear of the soul rather than self-mastery.

Being Inspired by You, Shining Star

We are constantly seeking out inspiration in books, movies, magazines, and our communities. Inspiration is the wheel that drives us toward happiness. We find motivation in little actions or in unassuming places, such as a flower growing out of the cracks of a sidewalk or a sparrow sitting quietly in a tree. In searching for inspiration, we lose sight of the reality that we are capable of inspiring ourselves, yet we often seek it elsewhere. To inspire you for you, ask yourself: What is appealing about *me*? What are *my* unique attributes? How do *I* stand out?

We *all* have the ability to shine. However, this also requires self-mastery; we must take time and solitude to think about and be inspired by our *own* inimitable strengths, our unique spark, while remaining aware of our weaknesses. To know our self, we feel empowered, not weak, and this is only driven by self-mastery and inner contemplation. Surely, we gain strength from the support of others who care for us. However, we must be self-serving to our needs and cannot entirely rely on others.

In searching for the underlying sapience of why we feel trepidation, we can transcend our weaknesses and not fixate upon them. While we cannot eradicate our feelings of vulnerability, self-mastery guides us to move beyond. Often, when a situation abates us, we avoid it or push it aside, and it eventually festers upon our presence—this is emotionally unhealthy.

Those who are highly self-mastered are conscious of their fears. This is a consciousness exuding confidence, passion, compassion, and power. These are the successful, respected leaders in our midst. They inspire us for one reason alone: They are self-assured without arrogance. Of course, many of us may only appear self-assured but eventually, our true self surfaces. Those who inspire many are poised with self-worth of themselves, and a worth that they attribute to others; their actions shine brightly and consistently.

The Sparkling Self, It Remains

Can you name people in your life that make you feel extraordinary and awesome? How do we know who these people are? The answer is simple, but complex. They are the people we like to be with. Why do we like being with them? They make us feel good about ourselves, and we remember even long after an interaction has happened. Years and decades later, adults recall school teachers they adored, or conversely, the ones that were unpleasant. Children are impressionable and especially internalize, and they remember the teachers who left a deep stamp of approval or disapproval that they may carry for life. Individuals who make others feel worthy have the self-mastered skills I refer to above, enabling empathetic understanding. The beauty of self-mastery is when we feel a strong inner sense of self, our compassion for others comes naturally, unconsciously, and is not mediated.

Enduring Action

For those we like to be with, there is one thing alone that sojourns beyond our contact with them: they made *us* feel good. The more intense the feelings of negativity or positivity, the more likely you will remember the interaction long after. Further, we like to be with people who can respect and appreciate our perspective, even if different from their own. These individuals are aptly able to put themselves in others' shoes. We can feel important in the smallest of ways, and we feel free to be ourselves. They

interact in such a way that they create a sense of self-worth for *you. You* internalize those sentiments.

In turn, this fosters your own self-mastery and a positive sense of self, which affects others *you* interact with. The beauty of self-mastery is it has the power to create a rippling effect. *When we practice self-mastery, we spread a positive energy that uplifts another, who in turn does the same for yet another.* Hence, adversity is the cornerstone of self-mastery. We know what it is to feel undervalued from those who undermine us. Self-mastery brings out our awareness of these feelings, and we are less likely to project negative actions toward others.

Can negative individuals in our lives create opportunities for self-mastery? We can be inspired by negative human and non-human entities on many levels. While highly self-mastered people are authentic and positive, negative individuals can deplete our energies. These are the toxic coworkers or friends, an uncaring partner who might break us down, an uncouth neighbor, a selfish sibling. These negative interactions form experiences powerful and potent experiences for self-mastery. The negative experiences only bring to the forefront the idea we need to be gracious. Self-mastery enables the articulation of negative experiences into a mode of what can be learned from them. Recall I alluded to the fact that self-mastery helps us to know our self so that while negative experiences impact us, we are better able rise above them.

Simplicity is at the heart of self-mastery—by simply being and letting be, we discover our innermost self. The highest pinnacle of self-mastery manifests when we make others feel important and we pay attention beyond our immediate self. Our intrinsic power moves us toward extrinsic rewards. Thus, self-mastery should be our precedential goal because it enlivens the achievement of other goals.

The world's greatest leaders and influential people can teach us about self-mastery. I speak here only in the capacity of my view of their success and influence, not their personal values. Whether they are introverted, extroverted, educated, or popular, without a doubt these individuals paved the way for us. We want to emulate and imitate their successes. We may value their achievements from a self-mastered stance. They have become exemplary because they were self-mastered, attaining their goals by being individuals of substance, by knowing themselves, their strengths, and their weaknesses in combination to the attaining of the goals.

The Success, Happiness, and Self-Mastery Balance

Why does success not equate to happiness? Success is an effect of hard work, but it does not mean one will be content and happy. There are many successful people across the globe with fortune, fame, money, and every material possession imaginable, yet they do not attain genuine forms of happiness. Happiness can only be derived when we build a strong inner foundation. If we can be

happy without materialistic aspects of life, then the possessions are an added bonus. It is our definition and reaction to these interactions that can "make us" or "break us."

Self-Mastery Guides Your Passion

In hardship, we stimulate all those aspects of our existence that perhaps we have not felt before. As I started writing this book, I felt a great deal of apprehension. I asked myself, how will I write three hundred pages between being a busy professor, wife, and mother of two children? Furthermore, given my years of lecturing to thousands of university students in Canada, my interests moved from research pursuits to building on the importance of educating students and becoming an effective lecturer. For me, this became the most important part of my vocation.

Over the years, I hear expressions of gratitude from students. Stories about *how* I touch their lives and assist them to understand *their self* in society are gratifying to me. I realize I am doing important work. I am helping students to understand what I call the science of social life, and I realized that I am truly doing something significant and important. In some cases, they have changed their life trajectory and pursuits because of *me* and a class they took with me.

As these stories increased year over year, I began to ask myself, what am I doing? As any educator can confirm, we care about the outcomes and learning environment of

our students, and I never believed I was unique in any way. In fact, being a junior faculty member, I tried to emulate and learn from my senior colleagues, who were far more successful than me. I felt a yearning to translate these stories into this volume, into a tangible book offering for extensive readership, one that all humanity—from the aspiring student to the entrepreneur to the working mother to the CEO of a corporation to anyone in between—could relate to. I contemplated for what seems like eternity how I would attain such a feat. My efforts had a sense of evanescence. I moved from "Does anyone care what I have to say?" to "I am touching the lives of people." Eventually, the latter won me over. I decided my story must be told.

What about my experiences and knowledge resonated most with people? I realized the message I kept repeating in all my classes, regardless of the topic—I lecture on art, language, qualitative research, religion, deviance, culture, education, and family life—I repeated the importance of self-belief, self-mastery. The belief in yourself is in no way selfish, but is in fact selfless, as I have demonstrated.

As a young mother, when flying on a plane, I must admit I become apprehensive with the passing thought of not arriving safely. I always pay attention to the emergency instructions, although I know air travel is the safest. Coupled with that, as a social scientist, I painstakingly analyze my social surroundings, sometimes to a fault. I recall glancing around me during one of the instructional moments before a flight took off. A few things resonated— adults are told they must always put on their oxygen mask

first before their child's. I would wrongly think of my child first and foremost.

Secondly, I noticed the inattentiveness of people during these emergency instructions. It was a taken-for-granted procedure whereby most people—myself included until I had my children—seemed to believe the instructions were necessary and important, but they did not think they needed the step-by-step procedures. They may have thought they already *knew*. We can all relate to the instructions about the oxygen mask; for parents, unless you have prepared yourself for safety *first*, you cannot effectively help your dependents be safe. In this case, it's an extensive metaphor, yet another motivational example about the paradox of selfishness.

The Selfish Masters

We repeatedly get messages of helping others, being selfless, and giving. But I believe selfishness in moderation is what sustains and creates our path to success. I do not speak of selfishness in a deleterious manner, but self-regard in a productive mode. For example, the Dalai Lama is respectfully considered a selfless being. Taking solace in isolation, he abandoned materials of a life of excess. Material life is often regarded as negative when compared to inner peace and lack of want, for those who chose to lead their lives thus. Admirably, the Dalai Lama can teach us about the positive effects of selfishness too.

The action of renunciation can be defined as selfish because one abandons material life in pursuit of the

spiritual path so that one can pay full attention to one's own self and purpose. Material abandonment leaves no room for diversion of our attention to material objects. While seemingly selfless, it is ultimately an admirable self-mastering action, and the essence of such a practice attaches us to our self and ultimately the spiritual realm, not materials or others.

History is proof of selfishly mastered individuals who have performed great deeds for humanity throughout the ages. Any great scientific study, invention, discovery had to stem from scientists, inventors, and philosophers who took time to be selfish so they might nurture their vocation and passion. In turn, by being selfish, they made fascinating discoveries that have altered humanity's path. Our longevity, our purpose, the way we connect with one another, cures for diseases, going to the moon, space travel, art in all its forms, the printing press are all the result of men and women who were locked away in labs, dorms, quiet rooms, retreats, the forest, in the desert, caves, mountains, art studios, space, and darkness.

My premise is clear: When we are consumed with serving others, we become selfishly beholden to showing others we care. This type of caring is driven more by the need for recognition, rather than care itself. When we do not serve our self first, we are damaging our presence. Our self-worth suffers and our potential to achieve great heights can be undermined.

This is no different from studying for an exam. For example, as a student, I enjoyed being with my study

groups and we learned from each other. However, members of the group also wanted study time independent of anyone else. While the group study was valuable, the autonomous study time was valuable in a deeper, more thoughtful way. Expressions of care through self-sacrifice of one's time, money, and talents are highly regarded today as positive. But self-sacrifice can be motivated for the wrong reasons, such as seeking power, popularity, flaunting wealth, or superficially caring about marginal groups to further a political, professional, or personal agenda.

Further, the cost to one's sense of well-being could lead to intense feelings of weakness and resentment. After years of sacrificing for my family and children, a subtle umbrage overshadowed me, not necessarily for the sacrifices I made for them but for the lost time. Time I will never have again.

Success and Selfishness

If you work overly hard to impress a demanding boss, are you sacrificing your own self-worth by manipulating others into thinking you are a capable worker, when in fact you already *know* you are? It may be argued your persistent sacrifice has demeaned you and not enriched your existence; we commonly speak of this in terms of pride. You become selfish in the process of substantiating *what* you are—your role—rather than *who* you are—your presence. Becoming consumed with the portrayal of what others want us to be, and persistently trying to please, we actually conceal who we truly are. How? We are strongly emphasizing our *roles* rather than our self.

The consequence is we devise a façade of *what* we are more than *who* we truly are. The practice of self-mastery is to primarily display to our sentient being *who* we are and *how* we are, not what we are in all our roles and relationships.

The dimensions of how we exist become more pronounced and are nurtured in solitary moments whereas, the what, of our existence is connected to our extrinsic roles. We often speak of "what kind of" doctor, professor, singer, neighbor. The "kind" deduces the person to an object, which is sensible if we are referring to their role. However, to think in terms of how and whom, we move our thought process inward to the spirit, heart, and soul of ourselves and the person. This finds manifestation in our interactions with others as well.

Think about how often we ask our children about their future: What do you want to be when you grow up? What do you want to achieve? What field do you want to pursue? These are all valid questions, but they insinuate a material standpoint. Now imagine what pathway our question would take if we asked: Who do you want to be? Who is your role model? Who will you emulate to achieve your goals? Who would you like to work with?

Transference of the conversation from an outward focus of *what* to an inward emphasis of *who* unravels the answer very differently. Value is placed on the subjective self as vital to the goal process, although note this is not

meant to take away individuality but to provide a role model, especially important for children. Feelings become central. Conserving the self as an object moving toward a goal creates a fragmented being.

Devising our existence regarding *what* objectifies the self. When the emphasis transfers to *who*, we retain a purposeful sense of self. In other words, doing well at your work is paramount for internal satisfaction and infiltrates our deepest sensibilities. Modern thinking of work is that it must be rewarding, not simply mechanical. Today, we are far too consumed with the what of the role fulfillment aspects of our lives. This has caused complacency, which transfers negative energy. If we no longer spend time focusing on our intrinsic aptitude, our inner self, we cannot practice self-mastery because we lose the ability for inward concentration.

The inner connection is an essential basis for happiness. It is a connection far too many of us are unable to nurture in the world of today. Self-mastery is only possible when the pursuit of our outward selfish desires to prove to others what we are becomes less important. This point is not meant to be regarded as a mode of mystical wisdom; it is generated from a practical stance. If we are focused on making our selves happy, in appreciating who we are rather than devising a persona that must be maintained outwardly, we will lead a more solid and real life.

With conviction, we must care about what others think of our ability; after all, we seek to impress to move ahead

professionally and personally. Surely, we must help others, volunteer, donate, and aid the less fortunate, and this gives rise to empathy. Self-mastery will uplift us to perform these actions with an *authenticity and sincerity that will flow naturally.* Thus, we perform those outward actions with meaningfulness because we practice self-mastery.

Failure to emphasize the self could lead to an existence of a selfish delusion whereby we become fixated on the action of showing care more than the thoughtfulness of the caring action. Self-mastery predetermines actions of compassion, kindness, and sincerity. We cannot express these attributes toward others unless we practice self-mastery and hold them for our self first.

Self-Mastery: The Pathway to Self-Worth

I maintain selfishness, not selflessness, is the requirement for well-being. Power does not translate to selfishness necessarily. Power posing by Amy Cuddy (2015) is a practice whereby we use our body language to empower our self in our communication.[v] Power posing is being "selfish" for good reason, presupposing us toward success because we display confidence.

Perhaps the historical ideas around the stigmatization of selfishness have created selfless disillusionment. Many social issues that manifest in addiction could be attributed to people who try to give unconditionally to others. For example, a heartbroken mother who sacrifices her safety to care for a sick child. In becoming selfless, one places others first, and this only diminishes their own self-worth. By ignoring our needs, we give a lesser part of our self to others.

In Pursuit of Self First

Learning a new skill is a gradual process, and self-mastery is no different, involving time and energy. How much time do you spend learning about an adversary, their strengths and weaknesses, so that you may attain an upper hand? Imagine if you placed even a small amount of this time and energy on to your own self. How can we endeavor to "know" others when we do not take time to be self-aware? Today, we have lost the insight into our souls with the distractions of modern society.

Undeniably, we are immersed in learning and mastering many, many talents. Think about a day in the life of you: How many diverse skills must you master to simply get through the work day? We are expected to have knowledge around leadership in a personal and professional capacity. We must manage ourselves and others, communicate, understand technology, be well read, be informed, be current and knowledgeable about our field. We become the salesperson of our self and must impart an attractive and well-groomed persona. The list is exhaustive.

From an astrophysicist to a nanny, we are all a part of this mesh of expectations. In contrast, how many times in a given day do you take time to turn all of your instincts inward? Because there is high demand and expectations for our outward roles, we prioritize these and ignore the inner dimension. In a given day, do you take time to

communicate with yourself, negotiate your needs and choices, and become informed about you? When we have not self-mastered, we become dependent on the opinions of others to legitimate our existence, our work, our thoughts, and our presence. As a consequence, our ability to do anything comes with a search for opinion and acceptance from an outer source. Undeniably, this is disparaging.

The individual holding an elevated sense of self through self-mastery does not seek others' permission to exist or take action. The highly self-mastered individual *knows* she is capable. Self-mastery allows her to exude an achieved sense of self-worth. Unfortunately, many of us stray away from what I label as the *self-masterization* process. Our Self searches and is in pursuit of the regard of others. We must pursue self-respect first, and in this way others will have no choice but to respect us too.

In the absence of self-respect, we advance a vicious cycle of searching for our self through the misled acceptance of others. *The deeper we seek approval from outside the self, the farther away we move from self-mastery*. Hence, it becomes increasingly difficult to bring yourself back to you, yet not impossible.

Social media in many forms plays on the virtues of acceptance by others; we may search for our own authenticity depending on how many "likes" our photos have garnered or how many "retweets" we have attained, and so on. We gain a false sense of assurance because we get attention through these mediums. However, do millions of "likes" or "followers" really create a happy, self-

informed, and fulfilled human being? The *superficially created* façade becomes difficult to maintain. On average, the working adult or adolescent spends hours posting and placing their self on display. Imagine if we mastered skills of self-knowledge rather than placing our self on display for others to approve.

I value social media, and it is a practical resource that is useful in many of facets of our social life. However, the point here is to show the use of any artificial medium to place the self "out there" falls short of substantiating who we are. The danger confounds if we remain complacent to the belief that technology could capture the real you—it cannot. In the context of self-knowledge, and while technology can assist to disseminate actions of the self, it cannot nurture the self. We seek interaction with others by placing the self 'out there." And, ironically this is a self that we personally may not know. These shallow efforts result in a lack of self-mastery causing a myriad of social problems.

The Secret to Winning at the Game of Life: The Connection between Self and Consciousness

Today, global societies are plagued with uncertainty and human fallacy. It is admirable that when there is economic destruction, natural disasters, terrorism, or war, people bond in a goal for the common good, to help and aid those in need. While everyone may not agree, the want for peace is a bond we share. Wanting to support, to aid those in need—we seek to help each other. What is the role of

consciousness in this process? Why is it we value making others happy? Such a nuanced fascination of fulfilling the quest for happiness refocuses our gaze. We are looking to fulfill *their* happiness *first* instead of our own. Why is it we value something even when it no longer serves us well? We continue valuing it because we find comfort, which creates complacency. This includes the comfort levels we have in *not* practicing self-mastery. Today, this has manifested in the self-destructive behaviors that pervade around us. We continue to seek medical, psychological, sociological, biological, and neurological interventions, and in some cases the solution may simply lie in placing our gaze inward.

What are the practical measures of self-awareness, and what does it mean to have an intense and deep awareness of *you?* Today, many acronyms for this exist, and we may refer to it as mindfulness. However, the path to self-consciousness has a criterion. To speak of self-consciousness without giving consideration to self-mastery is a false practice of consciousness.

For example, in most social science faculties, students often have prerequisite courses that must have been completed before taking higher level sociology courses. The introductory classes set the framework and guiding principles from which the higher level subject material will flow. Therefore, students must have the prerequisites to qualify for the next level of classes. These courses are the grounded knowledge and basis of the academic discipline. The general framework is provided, and later on guides the

upper year classes. Occasionally, students may be signed into my class without the prerequisite. In such a case, the student's performance begins with a disadvantage because the student does not have the same solid background knowledge as the others, but is willing to put forth greater effort. Certainly, the student can do well—personal initiative can make a difference. However, the prefatory framework creates an *effective montage* to draw from.

Self-mastery builds upon the same principle. That is, self-consciousness cannot flow effectively if the mastery of self does not exist first. The prerequisite element that provides the infrastructure for self-consciousness is self-mastery itself. Happiness, love, and sympathy cannot extend from you to others unless you are able to take the following steps:

1. Practice self-mastery.

2. Self-mastery leads you to develop a conscious view of yourself, namely self-consciousness.

3. You are led by compassion and empathy in your engagement, and these features flow naturally in an unmitigated manner.

4. Finally, self-mastery creates the endurance required for self-consciousness and empathy to coexist.

Delineation of Self-Mastery

How does this process take place?

How does self-mastery, which enlivens self-consciousness, in turn lead to personal fulfillment? The productivity of this combination of processes, when implemented effectively, is powerful. The result is an individual who embraces an attitude that allows others to do the same. The empowering of you progresses in a way that you attain the implements to empower others. *My hope is that this message provides a domino effect whereby if we all attempt to do this, others will follow and ultimately, we advance a universal human condition.* Work and professional life is a significant part of our existence and outside of family life, we spend the most time at work—thus, it is paramount to extend these practices to our corporate and professional levels.

The meaning of "professional" encompasses the spectrum of professions and is not meant for any specific vocation. Surely competition is strong in all areas of work today. However, being driven by competition should not be used as an excuse to emotionally damage others on a broader scale, such as in-office fighting, violence, antagonism, and bullying that can be driven by competition. Whether one is employed in a multinational corporation or the service industry, high levels of hostility do not give attention or respect to the mastery of self. Global corruption has manifested in economic malaise, civil unrest, political exploitation, and venality, among other factors. If we pay homage to the processing steps of self-mastery I outlined above, perhaps it would lead to better awareness not only in our personal lives but also extending to work and on a universal level.

Self-mastery is the rosebud, charm is its petals.

In the public and private realms, we are often drawn to people who treat others with empathy, positioning the individual with an "aura" or appealing energy. Why? What is charm? Who is charming? Charm does not require beauty, intelligence, power or success; these may add to the appeal, but charm can exist independently of other traits. Why do some of us have it and others do not? The ability to draw others in with our energy is simple, yet regarded as something far beyond reach because so few of us are capable of doing this. Anyone can be charming. Enticing are those individuals who have an almost subliminal capacity to make one person or a group of two, twenty, twenty thousand, twenty million, or even two billion feel worthy.

There is no secret or hidden agenda, yet we are continually fascinated by a trait so easily attained. History has shown that royalty, dictators, politicians, religious leaders, and officials can use charm for destructive and selfish gain. However, we have seen that charm can be used for positive ends as well: Mother Theresa, Gandhi, Nelson Mandela, Bill Gates, Johnny Appleseed, Martin Luther King Jr., Oprah, and more.

Being influential and charming is not about being well-appointed. It is not even about holding power. Charm exists and is an inescapable and enduring effect of one thing only: your ability to communicate with thoughtfulness. In purposeful communication, people feel your sincerity. And surely, there are individuals who may succeed by convincing others with a false charm, but this is inevitably short-lived.

Today, it is necessary to understand the role of charm in our interactions. Charm can create the passionate allure we have toward certain leaders, and we can grant power to the wrong people because of this allure, though this may be short-lived. In contrast, charm elicited by self-mastery gives life to an authentic magnetism that nurtures relationships in a powerful way. It creates the forum for which people seek to communicate with you.

Self-Mastery on the Lifelong Continuum

Self-mastery is a process on a continuum—it never ends or begins. It is a cradle to grave ideology. It may increase or decrease in intensity depending on the stage in our lives and the circumstances around us. When the Paris attacks in France occurred in 2015 or the Orlando nightclub terrorist shootings happened in 2016, people expressed how the events made them a better person by assisting the injured or helping their city to support those affected. These heavy moments in our lives are not easily forgotten, and they stay with us. In turn, they can also affect the long-lasting luster on our ability of self-mastery.

Being thrust in a situation of urgency, like the attacks, brings out the best in humanity. The strong sense of self individuals have when they have self-mastered is prevailing and is apparent in both harmonious and tumultuous moments in our lives. Individual spiritedness is communicated in many contexts. *Others* feel when *you*

have mastered yourself. It becomes a potent brevity commanding attention. We may believe this is the ability to be confident even in dire situations, but it is not simply confidence. Anyone can *act* confident or boldly. A confident lawyer, doctor, or politician can speak with assuredness and *seem* confident in their general attitude, but being self-assured may not be a factual personality trait that they have. Susan Cain wrote about the introvert, who may seem less confident but is still capable performing powerful feats.[vi]

The implication of self-confidence is complex. One can be more self-assured and have deep knowledge of their specific strengths. They may be confident based on apparent, and demonstrated ability. The *confident* person strives for personal goal attainment on a surface-based individual level. The *self-confident* person is nuanced differently because the *self-confident* person believes they possess the qualities to strive for success, and this involves professional or personal cooperation. The *self-confident person wants others to feel positive about themselves* too, while the *confident* person may only seek individualized gratification that does not extend to others.

What is involved in helping others? Does this deflect the responsibility for helping ourselves? We seek to help the poor, to feed and educate the less fortunate. Is it selfish to think we must care for our self first? In the Western world, we must ask ourselves in attempting to help others, have I done my best to help me? What are the limits of self-abnegation? There is no more destructive force today than self-sacrifice. Women especially become lost in the cycle of self-sacrifice and foregoing themselves to give unconditionally to their families and the various roles they play.

History has proven that the self-sacrifice of women has had an epic negative effect on our existence, our reach for equality and inclusion, patriarchal relations, and sexism. The knowledge of self-mastery has existed throughout history, and we can learn about self-mastery from many cultures. However, this knowledge has not been shared with women as vastly as it should have. For example, Leonardo da Vinci's famous quote, "One can have no smaller or greater mastery than mastery of oneself" has surpassed time.

Consider self-mastery throughout history: One of the first exercises of mastering the self through sexual fulfillment, the *Kama Sutra*, is a compendium on the art of love and passion from a spiritual plane. This act of self-mastery for sexual pleasure binds the subliminal and spiritual to the physical level. It assumes you know *yourself* completely so that you are prepared to give attention to your partner.

Our self-mastery pathways are uniquely different. We are born with unique qualities and do not emanate with prepackaged traits. The process of self-mastery is different for everyone. It lies on a continuum—no beginning, no end, ad infinitum. The effectiveness by which we will self-master will depend on our culture, religion, environment, experiences, values, gender, and even the climate and

population of where on the globe we reside. This can be contrasted to the different childhood experiences we all have.

Materialism and physical existence can support self-mastery, but they cannot propel it. It does not matter how financially secure one is, if there is no drive to learn and explore one's deeper Self, development slows and success remains stagnant.

Aura

My research on adults moving from education to work confirms that strength of spirit plays a significant role in the mindset for lifelong self-growth. Adults, who practice self-mastery consistently possess a heightened awareness of their potential. They have a better idea of what they want and how to succeed. Most significant is that their belief is their success is not merely a passing thought, but it is seen as a lifelong enterprise. These people can focus on building a worthy life which is driven by a strong inner foundation that must precede such action.

Self-mastery predicates self-consciousness because it is "the power to control one's actions, impulses, or emotions." Self-consciousness occurs after self-mastery because it is an "acute sense of self-awareness, a preoccupation with oneself." If self-mastery lies in the locus of self- control, we must be able to control our actions and formulate a deeper understanding of who we are—by our controlled actions—to gain self-consciousness or the awareness of our sense of self. Clearly, we need to exert self-control (what we obtain from self-mastery) to become self-aware (self-consciousness.) Thus, there exists a symbiotic relationship between these two pillars of human existence.

This can be pictured by my vertical metaphor. Yes, it is possible to stand on one foot, but with two it is easier. An extrapolation can be exemplified as: One must use self-control and discipline to come to know her strengths; humans cannot realize goals without self-discipline. To exert restraint is to control desires and delay gratification. Because gratification is not immediate, it implies hard work.

Gratification without hard work abjures a momentary nirvana that is lost almost instantly. With self-mastery, a sense of gratification is achieved from goals because there is deeper understanding of who you are and what you value. This opens the doors for self-consciousness; that is, one is able to exist in the present state—knowing who they are, and why they are performing the actions that they do—with assurance. Confidence, in turn, opens the gates for others to emulate and draw from this positive energy.

The notion of confidence is significant here. It implies and is related to *a present preoccupation of self.* However, this preoccupation is not a selfish obsession because it stems from self-mastery. Contemplation that emanates from one who has achieved an elevated level of self-mastery is a preoccupation that communicates the essence of shared wisdom and empathetic understanding. *Thus, the preoccupation of self-mastered individuals becomes the concern for how they can empower others to strive for self-mastery and the cycle continues.*

Often in the corporate world and our friendship and family circles, we are drawn to people who are seemingly humble. Such humility is admirable but is not accidental. These individuals are far and few amongst us so they stand out. They retain this position from great efforts and self-discipline of having self-mastered and then becoming self-aware. In turn, their awareness creates an appealing air others are drawn to, and we label them as "humble." As humans, we all want to feel important and have a sense of self-worth. Self-mastered individuals have this ability to make others feel worthy, regardless of their path in life. They stand on a solid foundation because they can exist by giving and empathizing with others, and this is their power. This power is cradled in the knowledge that one can give and empathize without sacrifice.

Further, by giving we allow others to want to emulate our kindness. This is the point where self-mastery can become cyclical. We use our self-awareness to extrapolate and bring out the best in others. While this position is difficult to achieve, education about how self-mastery positively affects lives can help us to attain this goal. Thus, we see a theme manifesting here: *charm, humility, and empathy conflate as the side effects of self-mastery.*

The modern world is motivated by competition; as we become consumed with outdoing the competition, we may remain in this mode indefinitely. It becomes challenging to

practice self-mastery because it takes the effort to redirect our energies back toward the self when we are used to energy flow being directed outward in the opposite direction. We are all striving for personal excellence. Today, our world evokes a kaleidoscope of self-absorption for practical ends. We are riveted with our self in every scope of our existence to prove our extrinsic value. We become the symbol of our talent, which we seek to sell for money and gratification. Our self becomes an object in and of itself, selling our ability and talents to the highest bidder.

Social media is both a positive and negative contrivance of narcissism. Societies today value the manifest display of the things we have. We are misled to believe that the things we identify with supposedly invigorate an "ideal life." This practice halts the progress of self-mastery. As noted above, self-mastery is a process, and we all have this potential; however, we must delve deeper to aspire to self-mastery, and the surface-oriented practices of today keep us from attaining the goals of self-mastery. In persistently placing manifest ideals of ourselves on display, we focus on visible relationships bereft of depth and empathetic understanding.

Self-Mastery and Universality: The Practice

As with all facets of life, we become better at the ability with practice and perseverance. An interest is mastered only if nurtured. For example, a child who has an interest in soccer joins a team with other friends. The child reads about the game, learns effective strategies, takes a keen interest in joining local soccer leagues. He is dedicated to practice and admires the "best heroes" in the field. The child's interest deepens, and unlike other friends who may be on a community team for recreation, the child finds ways to diverge his interest in soccer.

He may seek to coach and mentor other children or compete on local to national levels. The parents recognize his passion and support him. He further demonstrates his aptitude with determined wit and interest. Tenacity drives competition and opens the doors to greater pursuit of the goal. Through hard work, the child has choices of teams and activities around the ability.

The gift is nurtured and then becomes a product for personal gain. Eventually, the child exemplifies the game of soccer with a wondrous flair that takes him to great heights. This mindset drives Western thinking. However, the pursuit of talents must be driven alongside self-mastery. The same child who practices self-mastery while nurturing his ability at soccer becomes a grounded competitor. He takes an internally centered perspective. His game fulfills self-worth; it is not merely a game. He exhibits good sportsmanship because of his sense of self. In contrast, the child who does not practice self-mastery alongside his passion for soccer may simply be competitive. Winning and making money are the most important elements of his game. He may undermine competitors for cultural differences and possess an elevated ego.

We must nurture our abilities so we may remain competitive, to be the best; the goal here is to have people

everywhere competing for being the best practitioners of self-mastery. A utopian ideal, but can one imagine a world where we compete for who is the best at empathy or helping others to be their best? This is how humanity can serve all its members well.

The mastery of you will lead to a science of you, for you. Indeed, we can understand the process of self-mastery scientifically. If we apply the scientific method using logic, objectivity, and universal values to understand our self from a personal scientific standpoint, we can indeed predict our interactive outcomes. Therefore the premise of this book is to bridge together the disciplines of sociology, biology, and psychology, and to come to a better foundation regarding matters of selfhood. This is not a romantic premise. It is the science of the individual.

SELF-MASTERY + SELF-CONSIOUSNESS + PERSONAL FULFILLMENT = Empathetic Understanding

Self-fulfilling prophecy of mastery: We are a society obsessed with searching for talent. We want to master the various roles of modern life, technology, social media presence, our career, academic work, and hobbies. In our attempts to master many facilities, we have lost sight of the most important element: inner mastery of self. Regardless of the profession we choose, the interaction and relationships within the specialized context become paramount.

The power of denial: Over the years and from experience, I have come to identify the single most important emotion that undermines the practice of mindfully treating others well in the way we wish to be treated: jealousy.

The power of jealousy can ruin any attempt to place our self in the other's shoes. We all experience pangs of jealousy; it is an evolutionary component of existence. Social Darwinism would confer that "survival of the fittest" derives from competition in the natural world. Even tigers, lions, elephants, and other species fight for attention and yearn for the attributes of their fellow mammals in the animal kingdom.

Since the pre-Shakespearean era, we have witnessed many tales of love's derivative, which is jealousy. Jealousy is a universal phenomenon, a trait all cultures share. There is no shortage of love stories in antiquity about men and women competing to get the attention of one they adore. The sensation of jealousy can be unbearable if we love one who has rendered affection to another.

History is strewn with lovers who have given their lives or taken another's life for the sake of a jealous lover. Money, power, intelligence, and talent contribute to the rise of intense feelings of jealousy. Nature (biological predispositions) and nurture (social environment) can affect feelings of jealousy and the intensity by which it is felt. Jealousy is a powerful emotion, and it clouds the positive flow of energy and exhausts any attempt of self-mastery. If we are engrossed in others' successes, the materials they

have, the money they make, the partner they chose, we waste energy on thoughts fashioned with wishful clamor. Rather than enriching our own existence and nurturing our own talents, we ruminate on their successes or what they have achieved. This constant comparison depletes our own vitality. We must redirect our energies inward toward ourself.

Today, capitalistic and competitive ideologies of comparison are potent. To achieve greater heights, we need a benchmark by which we compare our self to and aspire toward. Advertisements display ways in which individuals and products are "better" than others of its kind. Thus, individuals use personal evaluation as a measuring rod to match what they have attained against what others have. The undercurrent of the message is that, while we may share similarities in the things we have, we are not equal because some of us have better *things*. This is consistent with the Orwellian quote, "All animals are equal, but some animals are more equal than others." We impart unfair differences on a materialistic level.

We are all equal as humans. Individual opportunities are politically driven by unfair practices based on differences of socioeconomic status, gender identity, culture, and racial background. Failure to recognize the sociopolitical aspect of needs and wants clouds our thoughts. The manifestation is powerful jealousy.

Jealousy can motivate us to thrive to great lengths and improve our condition, and herein we find a positive use of it. However, when it becomes all consuming, jealousy

creates an inability to self-focus. It impairs our ability to empathize because when we put our self in the other's shoes, we are consumed with wanting what *they* have, rather than appreciating what *we* have *alongside* what they have, even if it is bigger, better than our own.

Hence, how do you shift the focus from the other to yourself? I will share with you a practical guide framed by the powerful ideals of social life. These ideas and concepts stem from the academic discipline of sociology. Sociology is the study of human interaction. The ways in which our interactions make us *feel* gives rise to our potential for guiding personal behavior. Our interactions profoundly affect self-mastery and form the foundation of meaningful personal and professional relationships.

Time and time again women attribute failure internally. We are tormented by guilt, and blaming is the tool that lends internalization for anything that goes wrong. As a mom, I have had my own share of intense moments of self-blaming.

One day, when my little one went to school without her water bottle, I blamed myself profusely for being careless. The guilt was so intense I left a meeting to deliver her water bottle to her at school. The thought she would not have any water all day bothered me, and I felt I was an inadequate mother. My weakness was in my own lack of understanding of myself, not the event itself. If I had had a mastery of self-understanding— recognizing my tendency to self-blame—I would have realized it was a mistake, only a mistake. There was absolutely nothing to feel guilty

about. I was weak in that I did not have a solid mastery of my thoughts, and I let the worst of it consume me. Thus, self-mastery enables self-blame to float away. Gradually, we can reverse self-blame with the practice of self-mastery. Many mothers grapple with remorse because they lack a strong sense of self or low self-esteem precisely because they have been consumed by doing for others, forsaking themselves for too long.

In essence, they lack mastery of their own strengths and abilities. The realization of imperfection to make mistakes is a potent instrument of self-mastery. To master the ability to recognize our imperfection is to understand we are human. Too often, many of us are exceedingly critical of our self for not "measuring up." This recognition is productive because we redirect our energies toward mastery of the strengths we have.

We live in a world of fierce competition. Setting our self apart means doing what comes easily, but is so rarely used. In making mistakes, we seek to change our self, but rather than change we should be redirecting our energies to mastering our strengths and abilities. We constantly receive messages about the impossibility of trying to change others. We must realize their strengths and our own while accepting differences is the ideal message, yet most of us ignore this. Rather than focusing on change alone, we should nurture what is strong. We fail in our attempts to enrich our identity because we become fixated on what is wrong with others, rather than identifying what is wrong with our own self. Inadvertently, a weak sense of self offsets the act of projecting our own faults onto another.

Mastery of self enables individuals to search for what is positive about our self and others. We readily identify personal flaws of others and are usually hesitant to accept our shortcomings. Imagine being immersed in a social setting with a generous crowd. Who attracts your attention? The most memorable person is likely she who smiles, and gives a genuine remark about a talent we own. We must guide our interactions, so we gain a sense of achievement from them; this is the only way to flourish. Henceforth, mastery of you will give you the drive to feel good so you can do the same for others, improving their existence. In *Sham*, Steve Salerno notes we seem unable to retain ownership of our self.[vii] Its practice is meant to take ownership of who we are and not blame anyone or anything for our shortcomings.

Self-mastery dates back thousands of years. Indian society embraced this concept in the *Kama Sutra*. Sexual pleasure as an art form is mastered by transcending it to the spiritual realm. This elucidates the assumption that the lover who is capable of satisfying his or her partner can only do so through the control and mastery of himself or herself *first*. Intimacy reaches a superior level whereby the individual is able to satisfy the partner subliminally while the physical satisfaction is but a manifestation and outcome of the spiritual fulfillment of the sensual pleasures.

Pride

When we are in control of our thoughts, the smallest acts create meaning. From catching a fluttering butterfly on our finger to graduating at the top of your class, moments of self-mastery exists in all dimensions of our life and actions, both big and small. Consistent nurturance and flow leads to personal growth. This growth lends a better understanding of our presence and experience. How can self-mastery lead us to interact effectively with others? We develop a deep pride in the Self we own; a pride that does not alienate. It lets our being shine while at the same time letting others in.

The depth of experience: Have you ever wondered why you may go on an extravagant vacation and come back feeling surprisingly disappointed? Perhaps it was fun but did not touch you in certain ways. In contrast, you may wake up on a brisk sunless and snowy covered winter's morning. Feeling tired, you prepare for a long work day. On your way, you stop your car after seeing someone stranded in the snow. Knowing you will be late for work, you still attempt to help that person. After 30 minutes, you are on your way again consumed with a sense of utter satisfaction. A sense of <u>fulfillment</u> consumes you in the event that you did not foresee. This is the power of human empathy, and we are all capable of this. The gratification created is profound. You reflect and feel a strong sense of self. The thirty minutes you spent helping someone, developed your own sense of awareness that gave way to a deep emotional state of fulfillment, even more than the

week spent on an "in vogue" vacation. As humans, we subconsciously feel good when we help others. We all have this capacity and economic and environmental factors impact and alter our want to help others and empathize. Can helping others, in fact, be a selfish undertaking? It creates for us, a sense of appreciation, and we all seek appreciation and recognition. We feel good and recognize others appreciate our kind actions. This motivates us on a selfish level because we want for self-importance (Dale Carnegie.) Some may argue that our actions are unconditional and devoid of selfish motivation. However, the point here is to demonstrate that good deeds do in fact motivate us toward empathy. Additionally, those individuals who more often seek to help others are those with a strong consciousness of their own self-worth through the practice of self-mastery.

Self-mastery is not only action driven. Indeed, we can experience eloquent moments of self-mastery when we simply sit back, relax and let life happen. However, our lives are often busy, and opportunities do not present readily. It is difficult to control all aspects of our lives. Just as individuals prioritize exercise, eating well, one needs to place solitary times for self-mastery in order for it to flourish. The outcome is that individuals exude a subtle confidence, a generous humility that touches others intensely.

Empathy and Spirituality

Society teaches us we must value education, become experts, and master specific skills. There exists a clear correlation between highly specialized knowledge, skill, income, and rewards. These skill sets give us the potential for advancing success, and hence we are in an infinite pursuit of expert credentials. Today, we master many skills, from technology-based skills to social interaction and communication skills; these are practical extrinsic skills. Moreover, to thrive we require a balance between *both* extrinsic and intrinsic skills for inner feelings of gratification. Thus, we must practice self-mastery alongside extrinsic pursuits, or the rewards remain on the surface, lacking a connection to the inner spirit.

Chapter Three

"The seasons afloat, condensed into one. No barrier. The hues of emerald, sapphire and yellow become black and white. The blue sky suffocated by her splendor as the dew of springtime beckons." –Renu Persaud

Self-Reflection and Self-Mastery

It is only in deep solitude that we are able to find ourselves. In this chapter, I will discuss the role of negative emotions and experiences in the practice of self-mastery. Perhaps the obvious consideration would be that negative experiences undermine self-mastery and the development of self-worth. However, my research and observations have found otherwise. In fact, toxic people and situations could build resilience and in turn facilitate self-mastery. Moreover, how do we explain individuals who create pain and suffering, and what is the role of self-mastery in this situation?

Distress, misery, and grief have been written about, dramatized, and built into poetic verse throughout history from times of antiquity, the medieval era, the renaissances, Victorian era, modernity, and postmodernity. What is it about certain individuals that enable suffering rather than kindness toward others? Part of the riposte lies in self-mastery.

Certainly, technology has enriched lives, but it has come with a price. I believe there exists an association between self-mastery and technology and creativity. There has been a modern-day renaissance in writing and various

art forms. The production of art is increasingly tied to computers and technology.

By creating art on computers, we experience powerful measures of creativity based on the programs we work with. This gives many choices in the production of our chosen art form. Technology has allowed humanity to create art in a way that was unimaginable a decade ago. We are fortunate to have the innovation and choices to produce anything in a manner the artist might envision. In creating art using technology, are we diluting the process whereby the technology stands between the artist and his creation? Does this create a second-degree connection between artist and art form? I do not know the answer—I am only demonstrating that the mediation between artist, technology, and artwork is something to consider. It can have far-reaching positive and negative effects. Another example is the techno-savvy ways that we interact with each other today. Emailing, texting, and messaging are ways we can interact with speed and productivity. We can reach hundreds, thousands, if not millions of people at once. This has paced productivity at an astounding rate.

Can you imagine work or school without email? Yet not too long ago, educational and professional institutions operated very differently. In some cases, just as the computer acts as a wall between an artist and her creation, it could be argued interaction by email, text, or other technologically placed measure can become a wall between individuals interacting.

The face-to-face interaction process becomes diluted or nonexistent in the process. At first glance, this is reasonable when we look at society running rationally, with precision and heightened capacity in mind.

A computer acts as a wall between the artist and her creation. Whereas to paint on a canvas, to write on paper, is what I term as first-degree artistic designs. Beethoven, Bach, Kahlo, Monet, Renoir, Picasso, da Vinci, Mozart, Michelangelo, Rumi created masterpieces of music, poetry, painting, sculpting from first-hand listening, tuning, writing chords and poetic verses.

There was no intermediate object between the master, the mastery of the art, and creativity. Michelangelo painted the Sistine Chapel with bare hands as an artist on a canvas. No machinery, no sophisticated programs were involved. Some of these artistic creations still constitute the highest of cultured art that has ever existed. We pay an enormous price to own any of the remnants of these works. In addition, mass produced "copies" are cheaper versions we may find anywhere. This leads me to ponder the question, like art created on a computer, or communication by email, *have we also become a more economical version of our self too?* We must seek to understand the self, a vocation that seems to have been lost in modern times. How? We do not make time for first-hand connection, conversation, and interaction with the self. Our roles, friends, family, acquaintances act as the barrier between the self and us. The only place we can find a connection to self, depth that will give us a strong sense of self-worth, is during moments

of solitude to practice self-mastery. As an artist masters the colors, tones, tenors, and textures to capture but a moment in time on his canvas, so too you, the individual, must know those colorful dimensions of your life that spark feelings of gratification. Knowing the airs, the sentiments in your being which empower you (changes by individual), provides you with the implements you require to allow others to flourish as well. These elements trigger the personal growth of self.

Conscious Reflection and Retrospective Reflection versus Conscious Reflexivity and Retrospective Reflexivity

Below, I discuss the difference between the two concepts. The basic premise is that conscious reflexivity occurs *during* our interactions, while retrospective reflexivity occurs afterward.

Conscious Reflection: To Focus on the Other

Interactions become more or less effective when we respect an individual's strengths *and* weaknesses. We all know meaningful business and personal exchanges require a semblance of getting along. However, we need to know *how* to do so. Therefore, in the self-mastery undertaking, the process of reflection is limiting. Self-mastery enables us to act at the moment during our interactions *with conscious* reflexivity. However, this can only happen with sincerity if we have a strong sense of self and involve the prerequisite of self-mastery.

Certain individuals act with conscious reflexivity quite naturally and it seems second nature. These are the individuals among us with a superior sense of self-mastery. Think about those interactions which uplift you, permit you to feel empowered. Those individuals related to you with interest and regard *at that time. They* enabled *you* to feel your stance *was* valuable to them. You *felt* it because they were confident to allow a positive flow of energy, an energy they transcended to you.

Reflexivity is the process happening at the time we interact. Why is this important? In the moment, reflection allows the conversation to flow, to progress positively. For example, have you ever had an interaction with a boss, and then afterward regretted making a comment or were frustrated you forgot to make a certain point? Too often, we feel this because we are not interacting with intent. *The quality of our interactions depends on how determined we are to genuinely understand the other's premise, even if it is different from our own stance.* It is a state of accepting that you may not agree with another's premise, but you can listen to them. Thus, we move the focus from "my thoughts are important" to "your thoughts are important, too, even if they are different from my own."

Humans are very self-absorbed, and self-assurance with arrogance undermines self-mastery. This is different from the paradox of selfishness I discussed earlier. As with any vocation, practice enlivens confidence. We must interact with such fortitude that we become better at it. Our selfish tendencies are limiting for this type of effective interaction because our time to listen, contemplate, and consider each other's premise is narrower today more than ever. We are quick to draw conclusions if we feel overly self-assured, arrogant, or are simply in haste.

In a given week, some students may need to see me during my office hours. They may only have five minutes to spend with me, depending on how many are waiting. Over time, I realized the interaction must be a positive one. If I am to genuinely help my student, I must appreciate that the student took the time and effort to see me. For example, when undergraduate students seek advice on how to study for one of my exams, I simply cannot respond tersely. I often imagine the pressure they face, the reasons succeeding is important to him or her. *This is conscious reflexivity in action.* I have learned that the most effective interactions I have with my family, friends, students, and colleagues are those where I truly attempt to engage the conversation from their stance. They *feel* the sincerity, and most importantly they are empowered and driven by it.

This approach will always be effective regardless of the social atmosphere, whether it is from a personal, professional, corporate, cultural, religious, political, or legal standpoint. Conscious reflexivity is unique from retrospection. People who have an elevated sense of self-mastery can do the former well in both positive and negative interactions. Given an interaction, retrospectively we may feel satisfied about an exchange we had in the day. Other times interactions are tepid with antagonism. Surely, we cannot always get along, this is natural. However,

conscious reflexivity leads us to disagree and differ *effectively*. We respect the other's perspective, and while not a simple task, self-mastery elevates the possibilities here. The only way to show respect is by genuinely listening.

These steps open our minds while at the same time we are refining our inner strength, self-mastering. Think of a CEO who is speaking to an assistant; regardless of how much money the CEO makes or her high status, she cannot be effective unless she understands her assistant's perspective. If this was easy, then we would not require consultation for effective interaction strategies on the part of many corporations. Have you noticed the most effective CEOs are also the most popular CEOs?

Their skill lies in the ability to interact effectively at *all* levels, upper and lower tiers. This is an influence. They are positioned to permit employees to be empowered toward their self-mastery. To enhance our influence, we must enliven others' talents and intelligence. Those who hold power to influence need do so in order to affect the position of members positively. If they remain complacent and do not utilize their position to empower others, they risk placing their own self-mastery process in decline. This is the beauty of self-mastery; we must make others' existence a positive one so that we have self-worth, but this begins with ourselves first.

Thus, the desire to *want* to appreciate the other's viewpoint is a precursor to placing yourself in their position. Regardless of education, class, race, or sexual

orientation of our family members, friends, colleagues, and associates, we must genuinely aspire to want to take their premise. If we pigeonhole based on preconceptions, we lose the ability to empathize. Predetermination of others clouds the desire to genuinely interact because the interaction becomes tainted even before it begins.

Retrospective reflection: Henceforth, as with any talent, one cannot master understanding unless one actively practices it. Retrospective reflection is when we think about and reflect on our interactions, and this process enriches the mastery of you. Retrospective reflection is when we converse with our self about what *I* could do better.

Retrospective reflection of yourself in the interaction process will allow you to organize and evaluate your progress. Recording thoughts in a diary or journal, or simply thinking of interactions, enables an insightful analysis of your interactions. Here is where moments of solitude and alone time become imminent. Regardless of the method you choose, reflecting upon your interactions will lead to the mastery of you.

To exemplify, we often recapture various events of our day before sleeping. During this time, if you choose to keep a journal, you may simply write down your main interactions of the day. Ask yourself which ones progressed well, which were less than friendly. For those positive exchanges, what do you think *you* did differently? Thus, your focus is on yourself. For example, if you had an interaction with a colleague during your day and you thought she was being rude by raising her voice and displaying anger, rather than focusing on her discordant action, your focus should be what *you* could have done to direct the interaction on another path. I realize this may seem simplistic, but often the simplest solutions facing us clearly are the ones we ignore. We grapple for complex strategies, losing sight of the most recognizable ones.

Also, when we feel fear and anger, we lose self-control. Positive interactions require self-control, which in turn builds a strong character. Being wrong or right is secondary. Think of those who you admire, perhaps your mom because she has endured a hard life. You may admire her for sacrifices she made. We think of people who endure hardships as being strong. However, more than strength, these individuals have self-control that builds strong character. The character does not arise from how financially successful we are, or the car we drive or the real estate we own. It comes out of our ability to inspire others and not criticize, and seeing the best in others in spite of their weakness is what creates strength.

Self-control is the capacity to have willpower and restraint, and to be noncritical. Your mother may have endured many hardships and felt weakness many times in her life. Her strength lies in the control of her actions not to draw others into her despair. We may remember our mothers or fathers in the context of never letting the children know of their suffering.

Mothers are special because, regardless of culture, privilege, race, and education, there is the universal notion of a "mother's love," one that is unique from any kind of

love. We easily criticize and blame each other for our shortcomings. Most of us can relate to our mothers as being very strong. Why? We think of our mothers as remaining unconditionally kind during the times of their greatest agony. They exuded self-control at the most painful moments; this is the ultimate strength. Pride can make us intolerant to criticism. This alters our capability for kindness, which is difficult to give yet very easy to take. This leads me to the Self-Model of how we become driven by kindness.

According to the Self-Model, the only secret to getting what you want is living by ensuring others feel worth drives fulfillment. In turn, they too will be motivated to act with good intentions. Conversely, as humans we may be led astray, wondering why our kindness is not reciprocated. There could be reasons why it is not working: Was there ingenuity in your words and actions toward another? Your body language, tone of voice, eye contact, minute gestures are subtle ways to transmit messages. While we think in one way or say something specific, our body language may manifest a different message altogether.

Sociologist Mead, in his theory of self and society, advances the importance of subtle body language cues.[viii] John Dewey also debates about the fact that we all have "to be important."[ix] We thrive on acknowledgment. Think of the most thoughtful people you know—what is it that makes them sparkle? Today, more than ever, we seek self-validity and social media displays our obsession to feel important; Facebook, Twitter, Instagram, YouTube enable

us to be the center of attention in the capacity we choose to be. Individuals in these different forms of social media feel validated by competition for followers and the most "likes." Self-branding, self-obsessive behavior is not a past-time activity; it becomes self-imposed, daily consuming us with an engaging vehemence for attention.

This is shared by adults and teens, celebrities and unknowns alike. What is the price we pay? Is attention-seeking healthy? C. Wright Mills (1959) articulates this can actually translate to self-loathing.[x] Dale Carnegie (1936) has written about how self-importance validates our existence and is "our greatest priority."[xi] Today, so many years after his work, change has been slow. More than ever, we are enthralled by feelings of significant and arguably our need for this has amplified. One becomes "self-loathing" when attention-seeking action does not reap responses. We begin to question our potential by looking for validation even more intensely. Consequently, we are moved into the opposite direction of self-mastery, falsely assuming it is normal to require confirmation from others to feel worthy. Certainly, we should seek validation; it nurtures and motivates us to do better, but we must be aware too. The strongest form of validation is not from others, it is those we attribute to our self, independent of anyone's endorsement. Sadly, we do not always remember this.

The promotion of self-importance has become central to our existence, exploding and deepening to the point where we lack appreciation for *each other*. Rather than

seeking self-appreciation alone, we must remember an intricate part of fulfillment is found in appreciating others. Someone or something we detest could become consuming if we repeatedly internalize negative thoughts regarding the person or situation. How often do we get trapped in negative thoughts? We easily fall prey to them, but self-mastery enables us to push aside negativity we feel for our self. The secondary benefit is it becomes easier to do so for others too, but we must begin with the self. Emphasis on what is good about our self and others enables a didactic relationship between appreciation and understanding. Conversely, acting with ingenuity means our ego is yearning flattery due to lack of self-mastery. We become consumed with false sincerity and face value emotions for ourselves and others, creating a life of false intention for ourselves.

Why is Humanity Adrift?

Despite today's emphasis on selfhood, there exists a perilous loneliness. Even with the attention we receive from technological and non-technological sources, emptiness pervades. We are adrift and missing something deeper. The strength that stems from within and not one that is a showcase of beauty and privilege is important, yet we fail to recognize this. Today we are searching for happiness continually. Why is it that so many of us seek happiness—why are we *seeking* rather than *being* happy? The value of avaricious adoration in the public sphere is self-defeating. Surely, we thrive on positive accomplishments. To complement for a healthy fulfillment of goals is not the same as glamorizing self-importance. While individuals may grasp for attention by dressing or acting a certain way, this is simply mass-attention validation. It does not move beyond the surface.

At present, there are many unknown scientists, explorers, surgeons, writers, artists who have helped propel forth humankind with their discoveries and knowledge. We may rarely hear about the time and courage put into their work. They are not often recognized. Their action to improve the human condition is far more important, yet on any given day we may hear about the actions of those with celebrity status, what they are "wearing," rather than the artist drawing attention to child exploitation. *Self-importance, I argue, is only possible when we endow others with importance and especially those who are actually doing important work.* Thus, we must rethink what we deem as important on an institutional level from a cultural, political, and media standpoint.

Our importance of self only comes from the unique ability to appreciate ourselves and how we make others feel in private (and public.) Certainly, some individuals gain mass appeal for the wrong reasons. Their popularity soars but this kind of validation is temporary. A doctor may not be popular or have mass appeal, but his importance lies in helping others. Indeed doctors are important to our society, although most are not "popular." Our societal values impose upon us what we should and should not deem as important. The doctor is important for the role she fulfills

and the function of the vocation. However, the popular figure, who thrives on attention alone or has no commitment to the improvement of humankind, may obtain much attention. This is a fallacy of societal values that have us going adrift. We must rethink how we look at what becomes important and significant in our lives.

Pyramid of Self-Importance

Write down ten things in your life or community you consider important. To exemplify, I list five of my own below in order from most to least important. This will be different for everyone.

1. **Family**
2. **Writing**
3. **Friends**
4. **Work**
5. **Creative Activities**

My pursuit of fulfillment comes as no surprise as it is encapsulated in what is important to me; this would be different for everyone. Thus, my own self-pyramid would have, at the top, being a good mother and wife; second, my scholarly and creative pursuits; third, being an effective professor; and so on. One may define "family" from biological or non-biological relations. Therefore, friends who act as family may be higher on your personal self-pyramid, and the pyramid will be different for everyone. My point here is to show *my* self-importance is not validated unless I validate others in my life unconditionally. For example, in all the aspects I list, my

validation stems from my role with them; *however*, to feel healthy about their position in my life, I must authenticate myself first.

Graciousness

Taking the most unassuming individual and bestowing genuine praise can transform a reluctant person into a confident individual. With genuine praise, anyone can feel good about themselves. Over time, change is apparent, but this cannot be accomplished overnight; we crave appreciation—nourishment of self-esteem—almost as much as we crave food. The difference between flattery and appreciation is the former lacks sincerity. Sincerity is rare; otherwise, we would be much happier than we are today. Words strewn together like a pearl necklace to make others feel worthy on the surface is a simple task. The eminence to treat others with sincerity and understanding is rare.

Individuals who do this will always be coveted, will sparkle and thrive. They stand out *because they are different. It is a simple case of supply and demand.* Those of us who exude this type of understanding will soar to greater heights because we *are* rare, often standing alone in personal and professional lives. My ultimate reward would be that more people will stand under the wings of kindness. Perhaps we may get to the point where there is intense competition for helping each other to be kind in the human vocation of life. I deeply believe success lies in our ability to show others they are worthy, but only after we have proven to our self how worthy we are.

We become successful when we can find the best in others. Educational level, popularity, and wealth cannot replace this ability. For example, the most uneducated individual or someone who has no material wealth can become popular when the word spreads that this individual has a sincere appreciation for others. This gives rise to popularity and charisma where others are drawn in. Such influence is a beckoning that cannot be explained or measured. It exudes from within. Such exaltation is the consequence of self-mastery. Their graciousness is tied to the presence in listening and interacting as if you are the only one who matters in the moments spent with you.

The Interested Listener: A Guarantee for Success

I am sure we have all heard the saying "In life there are no guarantees," but it is always nice to have consistency. If we relentlessly treat others with sincere appreciation, we *can* be more successful. Ignorance to the awareness for the other even if we hold a high status could fade our authority quickly. We must be persistent even if to ponder disappointment. You may think "I have done this with no positive outcome," so why continue trying? I was once told by my grandfather that *to praise another when we are experiencing our unhappiest moments is the greatest symbol of who we are.* Thus, finding positive thoughts and words for people despite our personal troubles is a display of unselfish interest at its best. This is sincerity, it comes with no filament.

Genuine respect is shown in our interactions with others when we are an "interested listener" and appreciate another's standpoint. *It displays we stop thinking about our self even for a fleeting moment and think about what the other is saying and feeling.* We all sense this kind of positive energy; we feel it and do not forget it, because it is so rare. We thrive on it, yet most of us fail to impart it to others.

Often, the arrogant and selfish amongst us are not interested listeners. We have labels for these personas such as narcissist who becomes accustomed to boasting about enlarging their own character. Most of the humanity falls into this category. Oddly, the "good listener" is sought after because they are a rare breed. Think of how many good listeners you know. Now think of how many egocentric individuals you know. The ability to listen is simply lending an ear for empathetic understanding, one of the rarest of all human traits.

To empathize we must listen, unconditionally. Certainly, today our busy lives do not allow much time or energy for listening or even giving empathy for others outside our family and friendship circles, this is a reasonable assumption. However, we tend to think at the moment and for immediate gratification. An active listener empathizes with people inside and outside their immediate comfort zones. This pays off in the long-term. Gratification is not instantaneous, the rewards take fruition slowly.

Dale Carnegie wrote "people who talk about themselves think only of themselves."[xii] Further, he asserts

even the most educated among us are not "instructed" if they are incapable of putting themselves in others' shoes. Therefore, I do believe education, wealth, privilege, and status are the ability to empathize over mutually exclusive things. At times, the person with no instruction, power, money, or privilege could exude genuine compassion stemming from self-mastery. In other words, one does not require money or power to feel empathy toward others. Rather, we should seek to bridge empathy with wealth, prestige, and education, or lack thereof.

Giving consideration to the other is the only way to emotional health and well-being of our self, alongside its nurturance. Three general steps lead us to attainment of this goal:

Manifesto of Effective Exchanges:
1. I place myself in your position.
2. I understand you are unique from me.
3. I should not judge you according to my standards.
4. When I stand in the locus of you, I exert self-respect for me.

By mastering *your* unique abilities, you become a better you. We master these tools through conscious and meaningful identification with another's position but only after we have first done so for our self.

The cornerstone of this premise is responsiveness. Due to self-consumed practices—and this is different from self-mastery—individuals find difficulty in fostering

compassion. Why is it we have difficulty sympathizing and understanding one another? Why is the corporate environment conflicted? If it were easy, we would not require books, manuals, instructions, consulting, mediation, and conflict resolution. There are many avenues to help us become our best self. The Internet, books, blogs, counselors, psychiatrists, physicians, and teachers who offer services are in abundance; the list is exhaustive.

The Void in Self-Fulfillment

We remain lost when it comes to our ability to actually make each other feel wonderful. *Why? Because we are our self unfulfilled.* How can we support another's need for fulfillment? Self-fulfillment flows from mastering our own existence first. This is not selfish, but practical.

Today, this type of mastery is challenging because we are heavily saturated in other matters of our lives, such as obtaining realistic goals: the coveted educational credential or degree, climbing the career ladder, obtaining professional rewards, chasing a hobby, eating healthy, exercising. We commit to the actions of self-mastery in action, but not necessarily in thought.

When in pursuit of activities to conform to what is trendy in our society, if our heart is not in it, we cannot thrive. Rather, we must exude an inner strength and understanding of the actions we perform. Have you ever participated in something because it seems "cool" or "in style," such as giving in to a fashion trend, playing a sport, or taking a vacation to a certain place only because

everyone else is doing it? While in the midst of these undertakings, do you regret the activity or action? Apart from wasting time and money, we can be trapped by regret. Failure to think of our *own* tastes and our abilities creates emptiness. Imitating for the sake of fitting in can lead to disappointment. Regardless of how powerful, wealthy, or educated the population is, we are also more likely to be disappointed, and this is displayed in our constant search for happiness.

Why is it we have procured avenues that have set the stage for disappointment? We have high standards, and our lives are comprised of global networks and connections. Intense competition creates a pathway for disappointment, because we judge our self against others materially, not intrinsically. Many of us become disillusioned at our decisions because we are not listening to our inner voice. Sociologist Max Weber posits this as similar to our *calling.*[xiii]

By continuing to run aghast for perfecting the roles we play—mother, worker, boss, friend, neighbor—we *often fail to think about mastering the role of our Self. We conform to activities, act a certain way because everyone else is doing so too. This is the bandwagon mentality. Such a mind-set ignores authenticity of who we are and our wants.* Instead, living with intention gives recognition that our purpose goes far beyond what is apparent and immediate.

Failing to recognize the multidimensional self leads us to a meaningless life. Life with significance is infiltrated with encouraging others to be their best. *We can only help others master themselves if we practice self-mastery ourselves.* This is how our life gains meaning. For example, if you want success for your partner or you encourage your best friend to explore her talent, you can only assist these significant people in your life if you have a strong sense of your own talents and drive. If you venture to help them without honing your own needs, how do you even know to help them if you have no experience of helping yourself?

While our talents may not be the same as those close to us, we are better able to support others through self-mastery; this is what nurtures personal and professional relationships. We must all conform to certain societal restraints, norms, values, and mores in our unique cultures. Indeed, we want to be our best for our children, partners, family members, and friends. However, stop and think about this: Can you really motivate others when you have not the mastery of you?

Self-mastery is a lifelong process—it is fluid, on a continuum. We become better masters of our self by building on our experiences throughout the life course.

Ambient Mastery

A career woman deciding to stay at home with her child during the early years must master her new role as a mother. Women are often preoccupied with their dedication to their young family, and rarely do they seek recognition for all that they do. This is especially true for working moms. I wanted to be recognized as a good mother, but I

also wanted to continue the pursuit of my career. However, appreciation of my skills and dedication was but a shallow comfort because new mothers are often unfulfilled and depressed.

After achieving everything I wanted, I felt an ambient void but I was not prepared to share my discomfort with anyone; it would mean I was weak, not as capable as all the dedicated mothers around me. I believed if I shared my reservations, I would have failed myself, my husband, and my children.

How could I be unhappy? How could I feel incomplete? It should not have been this way. I had everything I ever wanted: a wonderful marriage, caring husband, flourishing career, and two healthy, beautiful children. Sarah was barely one year old, and my dedication to her hit its ultimate pinnacle.

I was convinced if I did not complete my PhD, it would have been increasingly difficult as she got older. I continued writing my dissertation after she was born, and the day to defend my doctorate at the University of Toronto finally came. I had family members who could have cared for her that morning of my defense. I chose to take her with me. My husband drove down to the University of Toronto St. George's campus on a warm fall morning. My defense was at 9 a.m. As we drove down Bloor Street, I looked on while hurried students moved through the downtown streets carrying backpacks, handbags, and other paraphernalia.

They hurtled by with coffee, croissants, and breakfast sandwiches in hand walking, to their destinations as taxicabs scurried through the street corridors and street vendors prepared their drays and tarpaulins. The fresh morning air—soon to be overcast—hummed with breakfast rumble and the strong aroma of coffee.

I remember walking these streets as a student, apprehensive but fulfilled. Everyone walked hurriedly to anywhere, which could have been a lecture hall, library, seminar room, corporate office, supermarket, and work. My husband parked in a half empty parking lot, too early to be filled–, and I sat reviewing my notes. It was 8:45 a.m., and I had fifteen minutes to compose myself. My child began crying—she was hungry. I decided to breastfeed her. I had to make my way to the defense, but I also had my baby in my arms, falling asleep as I breastfed her. Before I knew it, it was 9:15 am.

I was late. I made my way to my defense hall certain all my hard work had been in vain. I was late, my committee would be terribly disappointed and upset with me, and this was going to conclude terribly.

I entered the room ready to apologize and accept my defeat. Nobody was there. It seemed they were running late as well. Still disconcerted but relieved, I conjured up every ounce of energy I had and collected my thoughts.

My wonderful, highly revered supervisor discussed a few things with me, and the meeting began. In the end, I presented my work and everyone was impressed. As I think back, this day unfolded in a way that was quite astounding to me. A day I had waited for; for so long, it was *supposed* to be about me, only me. It was the day of my greatest

accomplishment but my greatest gift, and my child took precedence. That day was now infused with remnants of my mothering duties, something I never dreamed of happening. Life has strange ways of unfolding, but this experience was unexpectedly bittersweet. I would have sacrificed everything I had worked so hard toward, for my child. More consuming to me was that it did not have to be this way. I became torn and disappointed in myself.

Today's mothers attempt to conform to societal expectations rather than what feeds our purpose for our new role. Being a new mother cannot be a selfless role as we have been taught. How can we sacrifice our own existence for our child, or anyone? Does this seem logical? Ultimately, in surrendering our being for our children, women and men are not giving them the best of our self.

Self-Mastery Infiltrates Spirit-Injury

In fact, by sacrificing for anyone, we ultimately harm our self, yet we continue to do this. Women continue placing themselves second to everything else. Giving unconditionally as a mother, lover, friend, parent, or child, the condition of the absolute act is an injury to our spirit. Instead, deep-seated self-appreciation, not sacrifice, better prepares women to give time and energy to others more effectively. I refer to this as the *proficiency of you*. The only way to help each other, to improve this reality of our own personal lives and humanity, is to be our best self. Only when we are our best self are we then able to help others attain the same goal. The mastery of you is about

enlivening others toward their self-mastery. In essence, the self-mastery of humanity begins with each individual. In giving myself unconditionally, resentment held me captive, and this was and is self-destructive.

Self-Mastery Creates Winners

At the onset of my endeavor, it was not my intention to appeal only to those who are successful by today's definition and standards. We label certain individuals as "winners." Why? My thoughts have aimed to appeal to all labels we place upon each other. Everyone creates gradual and small steps toward success, and we are all successful in our own right, regardless of how big or small the endeavor is. Our definition of success can be as diverse as there are people in the world. *However, in societies, there are consistent measures of success that can predict success itself. These measures are what we use as a personal template for success.*

Based on particular societal benchmarks, success is conceivable. I call this the Win, and this promotes feelings of gratification.

Why You *Are* the Best: The Institution of Selfhood

It is important to be the best or think you are the best in order to set the mind to win. The mind is powerful, and what is absorbed informs our desires, strengths, and weaknesses. In creating patterns of thinking to empower yourself, your mind has the capacity to identify you are the best at *something*.

We are part of a best-obsessed society. The need for importance is amplified by wanting the best car, house, career, brands, the best children. Such needs are intensified because we internalize false messages that we need the best materials to be important. In our plight for best-ness, we forget those who do not have avenues to pursue their best. Why is it we require help to be successful, be happy—what is it that requires redress? The problem is that our thoughts are supposed to legitimate our social values.

The human body is made up of various systems. We require all systems to work effectively for an overall physical sense of well-being. Durkheim posited that malaise in any system or its parts creates unrest for the entire body. So too society acts upon us and is comprised of a system of parts called institutions—political, economic, legal, cultural, and so on. I add to this that society must be comprised of a new institution, the institution of selfhood. Durkheim stated we can, indeed, measure, because certain elements are predictable and thus measurable.[xiv] I often ponder how the elements of science can help us thrive and become successful. In our lives, we are surrounded by people who challenge us, who genuinely want us to be successful. But there are also those who injure our spirit, and as humans, we may tend to ruminate on negative situations. We fail to see value in the smaller successes. In a given day, we may have interactions with many various people and groups. The exchanges we recall most often can be the negative interactions. Why? Those who injured our spirit, dissipating our motivation to forge ahead, cause us to

feel self-doubt. Our attention should be channeled toward the positive interactions, but this is difficult depending on our personality.

Thinking often about how someone offended you merely surges their negative energy further. Self-mastery prepares us in the background to gain the traits required to transcend deleterious energy so that we do not ponder them. Self-mastery helps to arrange our mindful spirit to digress negative energy from adverse interactions. We then illuminate our penchant to move beyond futile words and actions.

Kindness

For the ideas of self-mastery to stimulate an effective change in your life, one trait is required: kindness. Kindness will give you the measure of self-importance you want. It will give you the fulfillment you seek. You will feel your best, and this matters. How do you exude kindness? A part of this involves the empathy equation I discussed above. As humans, we all have this potential, but failure to recognize and practice it leads us astray.

In sports, education, and community activities, we teach our children that winning is secondary, and it is most important they put forth genuine efforts. The attempt to do one's best is a win in itself. We delve into the competition knowing we must *try to win* but we *do not have to be the winner*. With this mindset, we release the mediocrity that allows for selfish best pursuits.

The mastery of you requires you master your needs, wishes, aspirations and dreams by starting with yourself first. Henceforth, the context is important. For example, if you are interacting with colleagues, the level of self-mastery is not the same as with your children. You may wish the best for a colleague who is short-listed for a promotion, but if it is your child, the *degree* of enthusiasm and empathy changes. By producing a relationship built on kindness and wanting the best for others, we become better for our self. However, to do this we must begin at the focal point of self-mastery. This can be understood as the *artistry of kindness*.

I believe we are all born to be kind to others. It is a part of human nature and existence. Individual circumstance may lead us astray in lacking kindness for each other. Think of this as due to the basic laws of supply and demand. For example, when clean water is not accessible, people must find ways to survive, and this can lead to unkind actions as people fight for a necessity of life. Even in Western societies where we live in excess, we are unkind to each other. Across the globe, there are examples of deeds that grossly lack kindness and humanity. From war and human rights violations, our hopelessness to possess this rudimentary capacity is lacking from personal levels to the broader global scale. Ultimately, our heartlessness has led to atrocities like the Holocaust. We have many examples of ethnic cleansing and practices that attempt to annihilate entire cultures and communities. Kindness cannot be given in the absence of empathy, and empathy cannot be genuine without self-mastery.

I write my thoughts about kindness with a measure of importance. We need to be kinder to each other. We will not thrive and live with purpose without thoughtfulness for others. Kindness allows us to put our Self in another's place. We may feel resentment for people who have more and think money, wealth, and material excess are valuable. Imagine yourself there for a second. It does sound enticing. Then imagine being scrutinized by media and public opinion, constantly. Do you really want this?

However, this type of critical need for importance from outside our self does not enlist mastering of self. Self-importance creates a destructive cycle. We enlist feedback from others to feel a sense of purpose from within. Self-mastery, on the other hand, provides you with this sensibility of importance, and what others think about you is secondary.

The Progression of Self-Mastery

What is the process of self-mastery? Actually, it is quite simple and complex at the same time. Frequently, we find the simplest tasks are the most difficult ones to perform; think of this as that which is the "elephant in the room." Seemingly obvious, we excuse ourselves for being too busy with life for silent contemplation of self. The mastery of you is the ability to put yourself in another's shoes; you are able to see reality from their perspective because you have a strong sense of self-worth.

You open your mind to unique avenues. This enriched mode of thinking only exists because you are a practitioner of self-mastery. Your thinking is not one-dimensional, it becomes multidimensional. *In giving consideration to your point of being, in addition to the other's point of being, your existence becomes multidimensional.*

Given a task, it is always comforting to have multiple ways to complete it, because we have a choice. Think of self-mastery as a GPS: to find directions to a destination, we input an address; we may have two options. We usually choose the most effective or shortest route. Self-mastery enables us to map out our interactions and allocate them to provide purpose in our life, for us and others.

How can you master yourself through focus on another? A CEO who interacts with a clerk may have various choices in terms of how the exchange flows because she holds the power. As we would choose the most effective route on our GPS, we must choose a route that will guide our interactions. The route may not be the same for all interactions. Often those wielding power can direct this flow and project feelings of superiority on many levels. However, for the interaction to be fruitful, the CEO can place herself in the clerk's position, ensuring the clerk feels at ease. In this way, the one in power respectfully obtains trust from the other. The CEO could also choose to interact directly, ensuring the clear message of the power dynamic is understood.

There are options, and with the practice of self-mastery, we can readily direct interactions toward amicable pathways. Henceforth, we hold the ability to redirect interactions away from the power-laden process because we have the inner strength of spirit. This strength allows for consideration of others' positions. To be strong from within renders us more willing to allow others to be empowered. On the other hand, we must question the supercilious actions of those who tightly hold on to the reins of power. The fear itself of losing one's power reinforces the notion the individual herself who has the power feels they are *not* deserving of it. If they believe it can be depleted so easily, then inherent here is that they question their own potential.

The personality who has power will retain it for treating others with respect. They win confidence from placing their self in the other's shoes. Assuming one's power can be used to coerce others into action is an ill-fated use of positioning. Coercive application of power in personal, professional, and political relationships cannot inspire others. It assumes a peeling away of a fellow human being's sense of self. Any possible success with coercive power is a short-lived one. If the single motivator is the will to use one's power to help others, then one's efforts are always rewarded. When power is used in this way, needs are met from all sides.

The Nine Elements of Successful Self-Mastery

The use of the term "element" is purposeful here because it has a scientific cognizance in that it supposes there are parts to be pieced together. The scientific understanding of success can be elucidated by knowing

science is meant to be objective, with universality and applicability to nature. Utilizing the organic metaphor, sociologist Émile Durkheim advances the idea that society is a system of parts that must work in harmony toward equilibrium.[xv] I extend this metaphor to help us understand how the elements of success in one's life work in synergy and are similar to a scientific state of equilibrium. This process can ultimately help to guide the practice of self-mastery.

The laws of science: Principles such as hypothesizing, experimentation, testing, predictability, universality, observation, analysis, validity, and reliability are attributes of scientific inquiry, seeking truths. With this line of argument, we can have a scientific formulation or a law of success for the mastery of you.

I refer to this as the *Self-Mastery Law of Success*.

An important component of sociology is the application of science to understand society, hence social science. Here I extend the science of society to include the science of self-mastery. However, is this even possible? How can we measure and analyze society scientifically? After all, society is dynamic, in constant change, evolving and molding. Every individual is complex, with their own set of emotions and experiences. What is consistent or scientifically observable about self-mastery?

The traditional sociologist Durkheim suggests accurately that we can observe society with the lens of science.[xvi] Fear, rejection, sorrow, love, happiness, death, life, anger, fear, heartbreak, illness, love-making, loneliness, marriage, procreation, sex, and life, are dimensions of social life found in most societies on earth. Hence, these are the constants in societies. How can we measure these attributes when society is undergoing change at every second of every day? There is only one constant to society, and that is change, a point referred to by Durkheim as social dynamics (in contrast to social statics). Change can enrich lives because it requires new ways of thinking. Today, it is clearly evident our interactions are laden with a benefit imperative; according to social exchange theory, we act with the mindset that our actions should have mutual benefit. In the practice of self-mastery, we think of our self first, and this allows consideration of others alongside our self. Observable and universal about self-mastered individuals: they act with unfettered kindness toward others, having knowledge of themselves first. This is the multidimensional element of action I discussed above.

We have all experienced adversity at some time or another; whether one is a powerful political leader or charismatic celebrity, there is always the template of the one person who thought you "could not." This person affixes their presence in a memorable slot of our psyche. And despite many believing in you and your successes, the one our inner voice festers on is the one voice saying "you cannot." We often falsely believe such comments because we think, can they be *correct*? You may convince yourself it *is* too difficult, you do not have enough money, you do not have the potential or economic or influential resources, and *they* might be correct.

However, think about this: look up the biographies of Bill Gates, Oprah, Muhammad Ali, or other influential figures—the history of their success is highlighted by adversity. Adversity holds our hand to walk us further and stronger. What motivated the success of these idols? Why are they some of the most powerful in the world? I am not by any means an expert in the biographies of these admirable leaders, but I can assert their paths were scattered with struggles they moved beyond. This is respectable. They thrived on difficulty, they moved beyond the "I cannot" to "I did!"

Think of your present reality; how would you measure your success? Were there people who thought you could not? No matter what you did, these individuals *would not* appreciate your value. Ultimately, we must be grateful to those who did not appreciate our potential, and herein is the nugget of a powerful irony. Had they *not* believed in us, we may not have reached toward the stars. Both the positive and negative interactions unite us to ourselves in powerful ways that propel self-mastery. Self-mastery at its pinnacle is comprised of both adverse and prosperous experiences. We cannot grow and enrich our existence with one kind of experience. We require the bitter and the sweet to appreciate life and what is meaningful. How can we appreciate the sweet without knowing the pungent taste of bitterness?

The Power of Self-Reflection

In a world where we are consumed with pleasing others with the speck of the possibility we may gain something from them, we fail to stop and simply reflect on our innermost self, our thoughts, our actions, and the effects of our feelings on our psyche.

Self-reflection is about making yourself better for *you*, not for the other. However, self-reflection must also include a mindset capable of placing yourself in another's position. A strong self will motivate us to help others to do the same. Currently, we fail desperately at this. Our world is a force for sacrificing of our time in the hopes that we may attain something from someone.

If you spend this time on yourself, you can do more for you. Ultimately, we are the sole source of our success, but we often underestimate this point. Of course, one is required to do the obvious—network, build relationships— allowing people to know you are out there. However, throughout history, the most "successful" individuals worked in isolation. They knew what they wanted and what they must do to get it. Age-old geniuses—Ramanujan, Newton, Galileo, Proust, Tesla—did not necessarily network or make connections early on in their pursuit of genius. They contemplated in isolation and the creativity flowed. There is much to be <u>learned</u> from the Buddhist ideology of mindfulness. The Dalai Lama does not network per se, but meditates, leaving material life behind. We may conclude they are very successful because they have reached the peaks of self-actualization. We can be

successful using silence and understanding. This is the power of awareness and self-reflection.

Chapter Four: The Art of You
Amongst all, you must love yourself first.
–Renu Persaud

Evanescence

To love the self ultimately creates a collective evanescence that moves beyond borders. Insofar as self-mastery is a process, we must make it a habit. When instilled early on, the potential to thrive and gain proficiency is strong. If children form positive study habits at a young age, it propels their interest in studying. The task of studying becomes habitual and less onerous.

Playing an instrument, such as the piano, violin, clarinet, flute, cello are symbolic of creativity which enlivens self-mastery. So too, participation in sports such as hockey, soccer, baseball can all lead to self-mastery. How? I was fortunate to have been one of three students chosen in grade four for the school orchestra. For many years, including elementary and middle school, I was a dedicated student of the viola.

Often I reminisce about this experience with family, friends, and complete strangers; I loved the experiences of my mid-school years, which seems lost in translation for many of us. For me this was not the case. Rising at 6 a.m. to be at orchestra practice by 7 a.m. on Monday, Tuesday, and Friday mornings was odd for a child as young as I was.

The Sun, Moon, and Stars

I recall my mother's soft nudging under my lush blanket, encouraging me to awaken. On a given wintry morning, if I was fortunate, I would awaken to witness the rising of the sun, morning breaking over the balcony of our house. Hard against the unripe dawn, the sun slowly peered through majestically, rising higher, brighter and stronger from far behind the climbing trees. Outside my window, the trees seemed sleepy, weighed down from waiting for the limber icicled branches to begin melting. Beyond, farther down the street, grand buildings surrounded by stone cold fibers would begin passing the shadows as dawn rose. Elongated steeples and the still lamp-lighted streets lining the black concrete road in the horizon, seemingly lonesome, would begin to brighten.

The best mornings were the ones that I stared as an onlooker to the meeting of the sun and moon as they greeted each other in the dusky dawn sky. I was intrigued by this scene, for I remember a story told to me by my grandmother. I believed this was the reason I was forever taken with the daily momentary affront of the seconds in time when the dusk meets dawn. It happens every day of our lives, yet how many of us actually witness it?

The stars in my grandmother's story were the sun and moon. I remember as a child asking her, "How did the sun and moon get there, so high in the sky?" She replied as most grandmothers would, with a loving and poignant myth.

As I recall, it went something like this: There was a young brother and sister who were very poor. They were told by an oracle in disguise to bring food for their blind parents, but they could not eat the food or they would be punished. They searched deep in the forest. Exhausted, the little girl complied and brought berries to her parents; thus, the oracle destined her to shine brightly and forever in the sky, giving light to darkness. She became the moon. Her brother, who ate the berries he found, was punished by the oracle to forever burn in the sky. He was fated to a blazing existence for not sacrificing his own selfish needs. He became the sun.

This story affected me in many ways; it gave the false supposition that the girl was doomed to self-sacrifice for her correct action, and the boy was relegated to heated strength for his wrong action. Although I know this was not my grandmother's implied message, it stayed with me, many years beyond her mortality. In my then six-year-old mind, I assumed and believed that self-sacrifice created a wondrous destiny, and we shine and dazzle in it.

As I internalized the teaching, I wanted to conform to the expectations. Years later, I thought about the lack of logic in the story. I made sense of the story repeatedly. Over time, I took the initiative to internally challenge why this story had the girl, and not the boy, sacrificing. It helped me to see things outside of "normal." In the process, I challenged mainstream assumptions, albeit to myself. Nevertheless, I was reacting with deep searching and analysis of my soul; I was practicing self-mastery by thinking and making sense of the story. I thought how applicable and practical this would be today; that is, the implied metaphor of sacrifice. It holds a profound impact on my life, to challenge and create other possibilities, not simply those we are "destined" for.

Over the years, arising for orchestra practice, this morning ritual of bearing witness to the conversation of sun and sometimes moon with the sky was when I retreated to childhood moments of self-mastery; it became my custom.

Harnessing Self-Mastery

We all need to strive toward self-mastery; the earlier we hone this action, the stronger we become. Without it, life becomes a challenge. The following is how I describe what happens when we do not pursue this path:

Life happens as if we are trying to run when we have not learned to walk. -Renu Persaud

How can we genuinely enrich the lives of others if we are not fulfilled? From an evolutionary stance, humans are not programmed to be altruistic, and to be that way would be an act of imposition. We must meet our needs first.

I remember that when my child was barely eight months old, I would allow her to sleep for hours longer so that I could keep napping. This was selfish, because I was sleep-deprived. It was about me, not necessarily what was best for her. Most parents do their best, but at some point we will feel weak. Perhaps we must rethink parenthood, whereby the best parents nourish themselves alongside their baby. In the long run, this will create a more effective parenting style, rather than ones with embedded sacrifice and resentment.

The result of forgetting our self is that we actually give to others a second-rate self. *This* is selfish. It took me many years to realize I had to care for me, *for* my own children. In addition, "independent" action will nourish the Self while others may deplete it. For example, in solitude, can I expect to nurture self-mastery if I am still switched on to my other roles, if in *my* time I check work email or run an errand? There is nothing wrong with productivity, but these acts are not about inner pursuits of the Self. They are about things such as writing an email or completing an errand; we want to accomplish a material goal. The desires we have stem from outside the self, where we are looking to get something accomplished. *What about accomplishing nothing?* Self-mastery is about accomplishing you and *authenticating you.*

The Science of Self-Mastery and the Unlearning of You

In my view and arguably, self-mastery can be likened to a scientific, objective, and universal undertaking. Indeed, we can predict who in our lives are advanced self "leaders" or not. At closer observation, we easily recognize people who are successful masters of self. Their power is garnered to help others with unrelenting compassion.

We can predict and generalize that from observation, these people enrich lives of others precisely because they have taken the time toward self-mastery. Their actions

create similar positive results and generalizability, as in scientific terms, is possible. This is the message I wish to disseminate here. Adversity is the ultimate motivator and tool for self-mastery to thrive. Reflection upon things that are not going well enables growth and understanding of inner strength.

It was a bittersweet time when my precious angel, my first child, was wrapped in my arms. Suddenly, I could not find words to express love, fulfillment, or happiness. I questioned every turn, the angst of right from wrong. What I was told, to be natural, was so difficult. Was I frail, incapable, a failure? I did not understand. Silence and insolent isolation prevailed as I stared at my babe for hours clamped in days. The wonder of her beauty juxtaposed the malaise of my inability. Staring, staring, again and again. Then I slept. My own rest and comfort sacrificed happily so I might fill my eyes with my baby. Hours later, I looked to the sky, then to my baby again. Tears, frustration, and fear filled my soul with the menacing hindrance of defeat in an untold tale. How could I be so talented in many facets, yet incapable elsewhere? A morose state of contempt disenchanted my existence.

The Limits of Selflessness

I refer to selfish empathy as giving fully to others, so much so that we convince our own self we are kind, not selfish. While this may sound almost counterintuitive, it is not. Drawing from my example above, I was serving my selfish need to prove to myself that I am a good mother.

My selflessness as a mother was driven by fear of defeat; I had to sacrifice, because this was how society wanted me to be as a mother. My pleasing was not self-driven, as I played into the hands of outer expectations.

In contrast to selfish empathy, internal empathy represents the most important empathetic formulation of all. Compassion for yourself, being good to you, taking the role of yourself for yourself constitutes this type of empathy. And in the process of loving yourself, feeling good, you create an aura whereby your positive energy reverberates to others. In feeling good about yourself, you naturally become more empathetic of others, thus empowering them too. Have you noticed how much easier it is to help others who are experiencing some stress when you are having a good week?

It is a cycle: we must feel good to help others feel good, and this is the only way that we can remove the modern-day ills of humanity that continue to plague us. This is a powerful mindset. We must know our own personal destructive traits that disallow us from empathizing with ourselves. Drugs, alcohol, stress, isolation, and alienation are the results of not paying attention to the self. If the mind is consumed with negative thoughts, you are harming yourself. You must first be empathetic inwardly so you may be kind to others. *If you are not capable of nurturing yourself, shall I ask the question, how can you be capable of nurturing others?* Therefore, in order for us to have empathy for others, we require an inner voice to reiterate this message. To remain

healthy for my loved ones, I must nourish my own soul first. I must take care of myself. This is actually parallel to our modern-day practice of self-absorption because in not caring for our self, we do not give our loved ones the best of us. We set the stage to further our success—for example, having successful children—when we are emotionally healthy. This is the ultimate practice of empathetic understanding.

Much sociological analysis is about taking the role of the other, but I add to this empathetic pathways. Vents that allow the flow of positive energy, which in turn allows the efficient practice of empathetic understanding.

Beauty and Its Bearing on Self-Mastery

At the onset of writing this book, I wanted to connect my greatest passion of art in all its forms to my ideas about self-mastery. I soon came to realize this task was not as simple as I thought.

On the one hand, I wanted to develop self-mastery as an objective reality we could all strive toward. I wanted to devise a universal reality that self-mastery exists as phenomena we must seek. Proof of its existence lies in the way we treat others. On the other hand, I wanted to connect self-mastery with the subjective emotions, sentiments, and feelings of art. The objective of art is precisely that it titillates subjective feelings and thoughts.

Thus, I decided to draw on the application of art, and use it as an extended metaphor to clearly articulate how art can enliven self-mastery. It became clearer to me that my

undertaking had very practical undertones. The choice of art was a useful one because we all appreciate art in distinct forms, such as music, painting, writing, sculpture. Art is anything that beckons feeling.

The beauty in art is an element of human life we can all appreciate. Regardless of how we exist, and where we reside, art is around us, far and wide. Beauty too follows a similar path, because beauty presides in the eyes of the beholder and is therefore subjective; the objective part is that we can all find beauty in something.

Beauty and art become infused when we listen or look upon a piece of art and *feel* certain pleasures. We imagine what the artists felt as they created and transferred a subjective reality onto a canvas or as they wrote musical notations. Essentially, we are empathizing with the feelings of the artist and connecting their subjective reality with our own emotions. Without a doubt, by feeling empathy, we attempt to place our self into the artist's reality. All forms of art flow from the feelings communicated to you for a sensation, to feel the artist's drive, purpose, sadness, heartache, betrayal, pride, hate, love. In turn, when we feel the artist's plight, we relate to the emotions in the artwork. For example, we listen to different music, depending on our moods. Why? The type of music reinforces the feelings we have in those moments that we control what we may listen to. I note that at times, we are not in charge of the music we hear. In music, paintings, fashion, we associate feelings that we can transfer to *other parts* of our life.

We make associations between art and our own feelings, and this enhances our ability for self-mastery.

Moreover, if we feel the artist's pain, surely we are capable of feeling the pain of others in our life—how can we not? Here is the intimate connection between self-mastery and art. We arouse our empathic potential. For example, I look at the paintings of Vincent van Gogh and messages of a mind in disarray, isolation endures, and I may feel for people who in my life may be faced with situations of isolation.

However, I was confronted with a particular question repeatedly. How shall I expect individuals to help others feel worthy when they are legitimately too busy in their own hectic lives to care for their own selves?

I was tangled in a web as if swinging on a pendulum between "I cannot" and "I must tell my story." Given the structure of modern life, I had no indication of how I would convince individuals that nurturing other souls, bringing out the strength and capacity to thrive in others, is the best way to feel worthy of their own existence. But art is an example of precisely that. With art, in a particular time and space, we *do* stop and feel. This idea seems laden with irony and contradiction. It is not.

"To be, or not to be: that is the question." The art form here is the written play. In one of Shakespeare's most famous and powerful quotes, Hamlet's soliloquy posits to *himself* what it is to be. Why? It implies deep thought and contemplation of being, to live or die. Shall we be or not be, and what are the consequences of being? The character

Hamlet is interacting with his conscience, unfolding the self as he ponders the gravest, most intimate act one can commit: suicide.

The Individual

The act of suicide is a desperate act of self-importance. How? By taking your life you state that no one and nothing else—disease, accidents, time—has that right over you to take your life; only you have that right. While suicide is a desperate act and a social problem requiring a timely address, for the individuals who commit suicide, there is a clear purpose. It alleviates pain. You are too important to live immersed in a painful existence. This belief breeds desperation. On a socially driven dimension, those amongst us who commit the most heinous crimes, such as crimes against children, can be said to also act out of self-importance. They unconscionably believe they possess the right to inflict harm and pain—they do not—onto our most vulnerable members of society, our children. History has shown that criminals can act out of feeling such a right.

Self-mastery gives our life the purpose of wanting to thrive. We possess the right to make our self and others feel good and not inflict emotionally. We unfold the various layers of our being for depth to understand our self. However, in order to do so, we must learn to empathize with our own self. Hamlet, in contemplating life or death, seals his fate in <u>favor</u> of living.

Is suicide a decision personally or socially driven? This has been a great preoccupation of eminent sociologist

149

Durkheim in his writings about suicide.[xvii] If we practice self-mastery, we gain the resilience required to transcend the measures placed on us from the demands of society, and that is why taking time away from other's expectations is important.

Shall I Send You a Handwritten Note of Affection?

To reap the rewards of a self-mastered life and its effects, we must also be able to personally exist and coexist with those we care for. What is interaction? The discipline of sociology focuses on interaction as the eminent and profound drive for human development, connection, and communication. *How* we interact is essential to transforming relationships and nurturing our self and others.

Today, the various forms of interactional modes have drastically changed moving from mainstay face-to-face communication to social media communication. Long ago, storied ideas of romance found lovers so desperate to interact and communicate that they sent messages via bird. "Don't kill the messenger" is a saying that stems from the fact that if one cannot send a message themselves, a messenger would have to convey news on the person's behalf, whether it was good or bad news.

When we type, print, or text a message, it cannot be equal to "in the flesh" interaction with one another. Is this possible? Humans give cues and gestures and speech intonation that drive the direction of our interactions. Technology is one of the greatest aspects of modern social life. However, with the use of technology, the important emotional elements of interaction have been immeasurably altered. Do emoticons truly capture how we feel? They reinforce sentiments, but do we also use them to hide actual feelings?

Rather than say or express our thoughts, we deduce language to broken words and icons, and we must be attuned to how this can alter notions of self-awareness. Are we in a comfortable space where we would rather text or email "happy birthday" than actually place energy into giving a genuine birthday message to someone we care about?

I often discuss this with my students in one of my Understanding Social Life lectures. As an introduction to the importance of human interactions, I ask them to ponder which they prefer, a texted "happy birthday" or a handwritten card. While some do not care, others have no issue with a text, but the majority often prefer a card. It takes energy to go to a store, read assorted cards, select one, and purchase it. Then we go home and write in it; really, one can spend thirty minutes or more. A text, however, may take a minute. Some of us may opt to write in a blank card or even create our own card. The energy and thought espoused creates an impression. Why is it that parents are touched when a child makes a card? My greatest treasures are the birthday and Mother's Day cards my daughters have made me, and the letters of love from my husband. I understand we are all so busy, and the quickest route is the one that beckons us; I overuse this

method of greeting myself. However, in thinking, really thinking of the profound impact the card has—if you care deeply—then there is no question as to which method endures.

Living Through the Eyes of Others

John Dewey wrote that we all have "the desire to be important."[xviii] We all want acknowledgment. This makes us thrive to do and be better. We love compliments, we want adoration and to feel <u>honored</u>. We want to show off our best not only in solitude but in *public*. While self-importance is glamorized, history is witness to many "important" figures who were befallen even with great importance thrust upon them: Cleopatra, Caesar, Napoleon, Queen Victoria. Great figures who get adoration take their own lives despite this attention. More current examples include Marilyn Monroe, Elvis Presley, Robin Williams, or Whitney Houston. We gain self-importance from the unique things we value.

In order to analyze the process of how we identify what is most vital, I ask you to list five aspects you consider most essential to your existence.

For myself, these would be being a good mom and good wife, and writing and having others read my thoughts, my family and friends, my work, my love of art and fashion, and creativity. In being an effective lecturer, I hope my ideas about society resonate with my students and ensure a sense of accomplishment for me. In performing these activities, I hope to be recognized by all of those

people I perform my actions for, *and this includes me.* My drive comes from self-mastery first, then extends to others.

Self-Mastery and Material Existence

We live in a society obsessed with practical abilities. We must master computer programs, academics, books, driving, and many other skills. In the process of practical pursuits, we become heavily focused on our outward capabilities. For us to succeed, we must nurture self-mastery because it is the precursor, our inner light that allows outward abilities to thrive. For any attempt to bring success to our life we must have a strong platform first, and this can only come by way of mastering the self.

The greatest ills which exist in society, such as child labor and sexual exploitation, violence toward women and crimes against human rights, can only be dealt with if they are approached from a take-my-place space. Self-mastery enables the attainment for a better mindset to empathize. For example, as a parent, it is unimaginable that my child should not have their basic human rights. When we imagine the reality and place our self into those parents' positions, we can relate to their plight. While it is not possible to completely experience the reality of another, with self-mastery we gain the aptitude to at least try to understand their reality. Devastating realities exist in many parts of the world; with the practice of self-mastery we can understand better when we picture our self in the other person's place. If we care, this is the most effective tool to actually drive the desire to help, and it starts from within our self.

Societies are in a "states of flux," and society is dynamic not static. We require courage to challenge repressive values that tangle our sense of self-worth. Audacity (courage) and empathy complement each other.

Similarly, empathy and anger can coexist. Often, we recognize exploitation, repression, abuse of a group. It is when we become angry— enough is enough—that we resolve to do something about the problem. This is empathy and anger working in a synergistic relationship. The self is empowered by letting others be, too, not repressing them.

Your Being

When we are in control of our thoughts, the smallest acts create meaning. From catching a fluttering butterfly on your finger to graduating at the top of your class, moments of self-mastery exist in all dimensions of our life and in actions big and small. Consistent nurturance and flow lead to personal growth. This growth lends a better understanding of our presence and experience. How can self-mastery lead us to interact effectively with others?

Henceforth, others' actions and reactions have a profound effect on the individual we become. Sociologist Charles Horton Cooley's theory of the looking glass self speaks to this point.[xix] Our interactions are the exchanges that give us the sense of who we are and how we are perceived. In other words, the nature of your interactions gives rise to why you feel pride, shame, beautiful, arrogance, and conceit about yourself. Through this argument, we are not active creators of our own

personality. Rather, we are passively receiving and internalizing the messages we receive from others. Therefore, we must act in a way that empowers one another. Further, this is not to ignore the principles of biological predispositions. I am demonstrating how powerful our interactions are for shaping who we *think* we are. Because our interactions have the vast potential to shape our personal views of self, mindfulness is paramount. The attainment of a goal is never sufficient. We require personal fulfillment too. We seek to have others share and be proud of our success. This fulfills us because we feel good by knowing our achievement made them feel good. I refer to this as the Win. However, to win we must be selfish, but we then extend the win toward others, hence the paradox.

The Win

Humans need to share their winnings, even if only to display and showcase our abilities. I refer to such achievements as the win. We should use the win as a springboard and grounds by which we give back, and make others feel that they can win and achieve too. Think about this, when you have attained a goal, won a competition, or in *any* moment of glory, what is the first thing we do? Inevitably we want to share the message with a friend, parent, child, family member, or colleague. If no one is around, we may tell a complete stranger or someone we barely know out of excitement. As humans, we are wired to share happy moments with each other. Today, we post a message almost instantaneously on social media, via Facebook, Twitter, Instagram, etc. We do not want to keep the glorious news to our self. Somehow *they* matter, regardless of how self-obsessed *we* are and how much we wanted the achievement or the win. Ironically, the win is much sweeter when others share it with us. However, the win can only occur if we were self-absorbed in the first place. The greatest cosmonauts, astronauts, geniuses, scientist, artists, writers had to be self-absorbed to create, build, think, do, invent, discover, formulate, design. The legacy of their selfishness can carry a $10 million price tag from Sotheby's for a painting from Picasso or a telescope used by Copernicus. Selfish time alone to nurture and hone, perfect, enhance skills. Remnants of antique telescopes we would pay for a part of their legacy.

What Constitutes a Win?

Achievements have the power to create deep feelings of pride. This is not a conceited pride, but pride that is fulfilling, more so than one that is consuming or showy. A win can be an Olympic gold medal, a regional soccer win, a coveted executive position, acceptance to an Ivy League school, a game of chess between friends, an undisturbed night's rest. It is anything meaningful to you that you have put *effort* toward attaining, and for some of us this includes good sleep.

I recall receiving my acceptance letter to the University of Toronto. It was all I dreamt of at that point. I was going to attend a competitive institution and have surmountable stress; I had to live with the thought that my delayed gratification had a purpose, and I had many demanding academic years ahead of me. Nevertheless, the pride and joy of the achievement was a win for me. Therefore, my conception of the win was not monetarily but emotionally placed.

The Win can be feelings of pride, joy, the high of the attainment, monetary or non-monetary. We can appreciate what it is to try hard for the realization of an objective. We also know what it is to fail. Inevitably, regardless of our position in society, we fail more than we succeed and that is why the win is significant. Very often we stop at the win, forgetting how to help others achieve *their* win too. We become complacent and do not envision what happens after the triumph. The process before and beyond the win is important because the win comes from a continuum of activity. It is fluid, dynamic, and non-stop. In moving beyond and using your win to help others succeed, the intention is paramount. Humans are wired to seek selfish gratification unconsciously, but to use gratification to help others requires conscious association and action. This implies empathy. The prerequisite of empathy is self-mastery and the fundamental aspects of personal fulfillment.

Our society is a masterfully obsessive one. We are all trying to become experts at something: our area of study, our work life, our social media presence. This is admirable, because there is heightened pressure today to be experts regardless of what we do. On the surface, we are in pursuit of our personal brand and selfish interests. And while generations differ in values, the common denominator is that humans must be competitive to thrive and be successful. By expending our energies in such a way, the mastery of inner self-worth becomes secondary if not ignored altogether.

To master our inner virtues requires time and great effort. The pursuit of outward importance has made us discount the sensibility for the greatest of all art forms, the mastery of the self. Today, the dimensions of life we claim to be specialists about are things *outside* of ourselves. This material quest is meant to show off our unique virtues outwardly. Outward gratification is limited and never lasting or fulfilling to the core.

Driven accomplishment merely creates a passing and momentary affront of fulfillment and happiness; moments that are but fleeting and transitory flash in the mundane schema of life. Our dearth of contentment is why we attempt to renew our talents and improve ourselves often. Time and again, we recede to unhappiness, searching, seeking for the next undertaking.

Gazing around your social environment, how many people in your life are genuinely happy? How many of us are content when we have mastered the tasks related to our outward personal and professional lives? Why are depression, addiction, unhappiness, and drug and alcohol abuse pervasive? The outward mastery of things around us persists and exists because it comes from sacrificing our inner mastery. After all, to become an accomplished individual, we must make sacrifices, and this is understood in the context of education and career trajectories.

However, we must also seek balance; as a global society, we become remiss, believing we do not need to prioritize inner mastery alongside the mastering of other skills.

In contrast, inner mastery requires we give to others to allow them to become the experts at their own strengths. Why is it when we bestow others with gifts, we feel such pleasures? The beautiful existence of being human is we *are* capable of embracing empathy, which can only stem from self-mastery. We give to feel "good." Self-mastery leads us to give our attention, empathy, and kindness to others without reserve. We feel pride when we are kind.[xx] Therefore, an important effect of self-mastery is the positivity by which we treat each other.

"Power of the Weak"

"Be Strong"

Roaring Whispers: Living, Learning, Working, Parenting

Be subtle, be self-mastered, and you will always win. Whisper loudly. What do I mean by this? It is a metaphor that implies my disappointment: As a social scientist, I can no longer numb my observations, having taught thousands of students, and having interacted with people from all walks of life. I repeatedly recognize certain patterns. Patterns I would label as sentiments like blame, anger, frustration, unhappiness, uncertainty, tension. Is it a product of modern-day ultracompetitive societies? Perhaps, but the other part of my analysis is that these attitudes act as self-destructing forces. We are destroying ourselves and others with toxic interactions laden with blame, disharmony, and frustration. These observations have pulled at my heart strings.

Across the globe, societies are inevitably connected. Intermingling with individuals and groups on a global scale is the norm. Our interactions occur between various professions as students, doctors, lawyers, engineers, actors, entrepreneurs, teaching professionals, professors, counselors, artists, and so on. Few of us stand out. As humans, we *think* we are important, and we want to feel accepted. Frustration ensues with feelings of unworthiness and negative modes of thinking. The result is tensions and internal questioning of individual action. There is a pervasive lack of confidence in self-belief that requires redress.

Certainly, today more than ever, social media has provided an avenue for people to build confidence around nurturing their talent and advertising their strengths. Social media has transformed the notion of personal branding; one cannot deny this. However, in the process, I have observed that something is amiss. Despite our advertising of abilities, our egocentric visions for ourselves, there exists a ubiquitous tension, a tension around the internalization of inadequacy. Despite our achievements and successes, we still feel inadequate.

We are immersed in a world where celebrities, musicians, athletes, writers, and professionals have

everything one can wish for, yet often they meet a tragic end. The legendary actors and musicians: Elvis Presley, Marilyn Monroe, Prince, Michael Jackson, Whitney Houston. One might argue these are popular performers who may have gone over the edge with the pressures of being successful celebrities. However, there is an interwoven thread in these cases. Reading the biographies of these celebrities, we find a personally placed emotional disparagement. Perhaps an inner turmoil and unhappiness from not being accepted for who they *actually* are. Instead, they are the muse for admirers and fans, placed upon a pedestal to portray an image in the public eye. Their inevitable demise stems from a lack of empathetic understanding from others. Wonder and success and stardom are short-lived and cannot take the place of being understood for who you *are,* rather than a celebrity portrayed in disguise for what others want and expect.

Inadequacy has given rise to audacious behavior that can manifest in various ways, from addictive behavior to sensationalistic actions to complete disregard of public interest. In the process of obsession over our outward self, even when we place our brazen attributes for sale, our ability to retain a positive self-perception still falls short. No longer are individuals capable of nurturing and being happy for what they are, or even what they have. We continue to challenge and want more for building our egos.

Self-mastery waivers, become nonexistent. I compare this to owning the latest technological gadget. We soon find out that, once mastered, we no longer want the gadget we have, we want the newest, latest version, and so on and on. The obsession with material upgrading finds manifestation with surface-bearing self-upgrades that do not reach the core of who we are. The selfish locust is not necessarily a negative instrument. After all, we are supposed to challenge our identity, learn new things, keep the mind fertile. This has given rise to fierce competition among individuals, causing information overload.

Our actions are not without residual effects. In fact, narcissism is widespread. Young people now take numerous selfies a day. Obviously, this varies from culture to culture, and we know billions of people in the world do not even have food; owning a gadget to take selfies is but a dream for them. However, in focusing on our own Western values, we know self-centered narcissistic behavior is not reserved for the West or for the younger generations.

Unfairly, the young are often blamed for being self-obsessed. We are all part of this ideology, which I label as self-affinity. Self-mastery is not the same as self-affinity, which is derived of narcissistic tendencies.

Self-affinity: This is the term I use for analyzing how as a society we are self-consumed for the wrong reasons, reasons that do not nurture self-mastery. One must be cautious in critiquing self-affinity. Ultimately, in getting that coveted position, defeating the competition, we are taught to set ourselves apart, to reverberate loudly. Today, we must do something to make our position stand out from the rest. Think about sending a résumé to a company that receives hundreds of them. How do you display that you are unique? This has maddened the competition between and among individuals and groups to extreme lengths on a personal, corporate, and global scale.

Indeed, today more people are recognized for their talent than previous eras. More of us are successful, and we pay the price with the expanding pressures of fierce competition. The result is a pathway of antagonism that has altered our mindset, placing the self for sale. As a collective humanity, we are part of the sale of the self-mindset duality.

Sale of the Self

Think about anything for sale. A sale is the offer of a lesser amount of an object of what was first implied it *should* cost. In the first place, we must question who even decides what an object costs. Karl Marx has brought our attention to the commodification of the self by capitalistic means. He posits that the masses ultimately fall victim to alienation. Similarly, Durkheim theorized that anomie, which is a sense of normlessness, creates a disconnection between self and social worlds.[xxi] Further, Max Weber also believed that disenchantment arose from modern societies becoming more rational.[xxii] These ultimately have devastating effects to our social existence.

Nevertheless, our abilities and strengths are saleable, and we must sell ourselves to win over the competition in love, in the workplace, in our communities, politics, education, cultural practices, and many other facets of life. We must provide a product of ourselves to the highest bidder and win the contract. The glorious high and adrenaline rush of winning a coveted role, contract, or corporate position is undeniable. We may have but very few moments like these across our lifetime.

I will never forget the day I was granted my faculty position. The sense of accomplishment, the reality that my hard work was recognized lasted for a fleeting moment. I was poised and very privileged to have lifelong access to do what I am most passionate about: lecture, teach, and research on various aspects of social life, which I knew well. The high did not last. Soon after, I was in pursuit of my next challenge. I wanted to have even more, when this was *all* I had wanted in the recent past.

My inner self was certainly for sale. I wanted to be recognized for abilities outside the realm of my professorial and lecturing vocation. I wanted to challenge myself further. The realization we have *all* we ever wanted creates an emptiness and yearning for more. We do not spend time in appreciating the present achievements. The high dissipates rapidly. Suddenly, we may feel trapped because "all we ever wanted" does not seem enough.

Think about the person you so love, would do anything for, they are all you ever wanted.

If one believe the traditional ideas around the institution of marriage, the expectation is that a couple is married to spend their lives together. Statistics in North America show that the odds are that within a few years, the couple will be divorced. What happened? In pursuit of our personal and professional ever afters, humans have become complacent. The will to practice self-mastery has weakened, almost disappeared in modern times. This has given rise to professional angst, staggeringly high physical ailments, mental illness, and societal dysfunctions, increase in violence, drug and alcohol abuse, breakdown in family life, and more. The lack of empathy and heightened resentment occurs from a lack of self-mastery.

We fail to make the most important relationships flourish not because of self-preoccupation but for lack of self-mastery. Surface-oriented self-interest has created a disconnection of our self from others in our personal and professional lives. How? Today, more than ever we lack empathy for one another. Genuine empathy can only stem from self-mastery. We are hesitant to put ourselves in another's shoes. In the pursuits of the outward self, we are creating, rehearsing, and refabricating scenarios where anyone and everyone will remember us. In the process, we have lost regard for how to make others feel good about *them self* while making our self to feel important from within *first.*

My premise does not deny the importance of self-interest in today's world. On the contrary, by paying attention to others' needs and being empathetic to their stance, we are actually feeding our own interests. But we are doing this in a more sensitive and pragmatic way; self-interest cannot melt away in the name of giving selflessly. That thinking has not eradicated the ills facing our global community, and in fact these have confounded. Therefore, we require a new way of thinking about the self. After all,

self-interest has given us Newton, Rousseau, and Voltaire, philosophers who contemplate.

Presently, we still live by their ideas. Ultimately, meeting our basic needs requires deep-seated self-interest. Society has evolved away from natural altruism and is now fervently premised on Darwinian notions of "survival of the fittest." Sentiment around self-interest reigns true, in the workplace, systems of education, politics, legal institutions, etc. I am advancing the thought that we require a modern-day shift in our mindset. A shift that regards attention to the self as an unselfish practice, because this can lead a global will toward a heightened awareness of each other. This is the ultimate success. Obviously, such a shift must be consistent with modern values. We must move our focus *from ourselves to others*. But how is this possible when we are all after the execution of our success and aspiring dreams?

Chapter Five, Summary:

In this chapter, I will outline what I refer to as the important elements of social interaction, which ultimately assist us toward self-mastery.

The Social Butterfly Effect
The Beauty of Personal Interactions and Empathy Building
The Self-Mastery Quotient

Self-mastery is elevated to the ultimate realm by interactions based on empathy. As with all things, we must practice with rigor to excel in the particular vocation we choose. One gains self-mastery with repetition, dedication, and concentration. For example, lawyers must article, doctors must complete internships, monkhood and priesthood adhere to a life of spiritual teachings and practices, and so on. In the same vein, we must practice self-mastery with the constant deference of self, enabling a rich exchanges in our relationships.

The constant interaction with technology, devices, and computers can assume positive and negative effects on the mastery of self. Most interaction in the West now occurs by means of a smartphone, computer, or other gadgetry. Not only are we moving further away from the traditional richness of face–to-face interactions, but self-engagement is becoming nonexistent. Alone time is spent by occupying our self with our technology and its conveniences because the technology has indeed improved our productivity in a positive way. However, balance again is key, and the problem is that we do not set aside silent moments for contemplation to think about our life and relationships. Often if we do, it is alone time with our device.

The Social Butterfly Effect and Interaction

I have formulated what I refer to as the Ten Rules of Effective Social Interactions.

A Constitution of the Self

All human interaction becomes social as soon as two parties are involved. Does the interaction with the self constitute a social interaction?

The looking-glass self is a sociological premise made popular by sociologist Charles Cooley.[xxiii] We develop a sensibility of who we are based on the feedback we get from others. However, we can and do interact with our own self; for example, looking into the mirror as you practice a speech alone. Cooley posits that while looking at your reflection, you imagine how others will perceive you. Based on this perception of yourself as you see your reflection, you then feel pride or disappointment, hence the looking-glass self.

Given the assumptions of the looking-glass self, do we ever stop being social and are we able to be our complete self when alone? This is a complex question with many possible answers; however, from a sociological standpoint, society *always* affects our behaviors, and choices. For example, imagine your roommate stepped out and you are alone in your apartment. You know your roommate is abhorrent about smoking and while you may want to smoke, you decide not to, and the choice of not smoking is an indication of how society acts upon each of us *in situ.* Our actions are contained in social norms even in isolation.

Interaction with self *does* constitute a social interaction because the self is comprised of two parts that are in constant tension: The "I" and the "Me." What does this mean? The "I" is what I want, and the "me" is what I should want. Another eminent sociologist, George Herbert Mead, distinguishes that the "I" parts of self are the biological, psychological, physiological, organic temptations, the actions we need to be fulfilled regardless of society's impression of us.[xxiv] Think of this as the Freudian counterpart of the "id." The "me" part of the self is the dimension socially constrained by society. We must act with decorum and give consideration to others, even if we may be uncomfortable doing so. Think of this as Freud's "ego."

Inadvertently, the decision not to smoke becomes a personal decision, but one that *is* socially driven from the disapproval of your roommate. Hence, even in isolation, we are constrained by others. Our constraint is driven by empathy because we continue to care about what they think, by placing ourself in their shoes. We become powerfully affective personalities when we own the ability to regard others even when they are not present.

Our busy lives make it difficult to be alone. There are many activities for nurturing solitary practices to connect you to your inner self. Alone time is essential; it allows us to practice *how* to be empathetic. When alone, do you feel inhibited, or are you free to do as you please, and to what extent? The lack of the other's position is regarded as apathy and can have profound effects on self-mastery and interactions.

Apathy is the opposite of empathy, and much historical literature is derived from the bleeding heart filled with the apathy in direct opposition of the empathetic spirit. Various forms of technology give rise to apathy because it can distort the empathetic process. Apathy develops through selfishness and attention-seeking. Gratification for the apathetic person is powered by disregarding the feelings of others.

In the following passage, I list rules I believe can aid our interactions to be progressive rather than apathetic. Apathy cloaked in unkindness to our fellow humanity is the root of many social problems today. The bleeding heart is concealed with apathy.

The Empathy Continuum

All interactions fall somewhere on this continuum, regardless of how big or small they are. Empathy nurtured by self-mastery positions us one step closer to the mountain peak of empathetic regard for others; it brings happiness, contentment, love and just plain being nice.

The Ten Rules of Empathic Exchanges

1. Interactions are social endeavors and include interaction with self, which *is* social.

2. We learn from all interactions.

3. We must have positive and negative interactions to build a strong sense of self.

4. Interactions impact us on a continuum from high to low affect.

5. Self-mastery acts as a pathway for fruitful interactions.

6. Interactions are fueled with both apathy and empathy.

7. We must interact with intention.

8. We must place our self in the other's shoes to be effective.

9. We must act more than speak; actions hold power over words.

10. Your ability to relate effectively is a direct correlation of your level of self-mastery.

Ask yourself what you gain from your interactions. On a daily basis, are your connections affirmative or deleterious? The more uplifting interactions are embedded with empathetic understanding—the person accepts your point of view, you accept theirs. Undesirable exchanges leave us feeling as empty vessels. At times it is the unspoken and more subtle forms of communication that can leave a positive impact or imprint upon us. How? Subtly, the interaction made us feel positive about *ourselves*.

All interactions powerfully evoke sentiments about self, whether we realize this or not. Subconsciously, we surmise the way we feel when we interrelate with others.

For example, going into a coffee shop, grocery store, gas station, bar, restaurant—upon exiting, we remember whether the waiter or waitress, cashier, barista, server was "nice." More than anything else, we recognize how they made *us* feel, how helpful they were.

Our interactions are significant, regardless of how intense they are; I divide our interactions along a continuum. The idea is that when we interact with family and friends, the members closest to us, these interactions have a stronger impact. Ideas of family have changed, and deep bonds are not necessarily formed by the genetic constitution of the family alone.

The Profound Power of Our Interactions on Self-Mastery

Care for the mind, it will care for the body. Mindfulness is an exercise for the self. To act mindfully is to give attention to the moment in which we are taking action. Concentration on our performance at that is a presence in action.

During exchanges, we can sense and feel mindfully-driven communication. For example, after speaking with someone we just met, in mere seconds, we may *feel* a connection. The connection comes from the earnest two-way flow of the interaction. In other words, we pay attention to the other and feel their sincere attention toward us too. In reciprocating, we achieve a connection.

In contrast, we can sit at dinner for two hours with a partner, yet the entire time there seems to be a lack of

connection. This occurs because either one or both parties fail to act mindfully and with concentration toward the other. Often we label this as "distracted," "lost," or simply "not wanting to be there." We feel these sentiments in personal and professional relations. To avoid offending, we must relate to each other with respect to their feelings, and this requires an elegant subtlety in our_behavior.

The elegance of power in our exchanges: Think about some of the world's greatest celebrities, religious or political leaders that we may identify with, such as the Dalai Lama, Oprah Winfrey, Shah Rukh Khan, or Angelina Jolie, names that are internationally recognized. They hold positions of power from their mass appeal and influence on a global scale. It can be argued they also exude a certain humble quality in interviews or when asked about events in their life. I refer to this as elegant power, a power exercised with empathy, humility, and a lack of extravagance.

The Social Interaction Quotient (SIQ)

Intelligence Quotients (IQ) and Emotional Quotients (EQ) are standards by which we may measure the intelligence or emotional level of individuals. I have formulated and added to these measurements our effectiveness or lack thereof to socially interact. I refer to this as the Social Interaction Quotient (SIQ), and I believe this too must be taken into account for well-being. In fact, SIQ may enhance the development of EQ and IQ. The SIQ is significant, because without the SIQ intelligence and emotional maturity could struggle to exist and be nurtured.

Studies have shown that social interaction is key to the formation of intelligence and emotional understanding for our self and each other.[xxv] Further, interactions that are enunciated in empathy nurture the development of the SIQ of the individual. Studies have shown that children who are isolated from the early years are not able to express empathy because they were not interacting with others to develop empathy. The building of one's IQ is strongly contingent upon how effectively the SIQ and EQ are developed. These three dimensions do not act in isolation, nor are they mutually exclusive. They work in a synergistic relationship. For SIQ to be nurtured and grow, as with anything, it requires practice in congruence with the other factors, and this solidifies self-mastery.

One can argue to some extent that while social media is a very important part of people's lives today, providing opportunities we could not otherwise conceive of, it may also inhibit SIQ development because of the lack of face-to-face interaction. I propose we must interact physically in addition to other forms of interaction for the development of empathetic understanding for each other. Insofar as social media, we certainly feel many emotions at differing levels and I do not infer that we do not have face-to-face interactions. However, the quality of our interactions must be considered. For example, upon going on one's Facebook page, we may experience many emotions of jealousy, disgust, fear, envy, or happiness depending on what is posted by our friends. We then judge people according to the visual representations. In doing so, our visual sense dominates as we draw our conclusions.

However, in a hearty personal interaction, all senses act upon us to create a myriad of feelings. We see the person, smell them; we may feel their touch, and so on. We are fortunate that technology such as Skype and other forms of social media allow us to stay in communication, especially with loved ones from afar. But these modes of interaction have also permanently altered the landscape of our exchanges. Could we argue they may play a role in a lack of empathetic understanding that plagues our global societies? I do not have the scope here to answer this question, but I propose it is worth consideration, simply to enable us to think about how our interactions could be reformulated to better understand each other. Essentially, this comes back to placing ourselves in that person's stance.

Nevertheless, as individuals, we can only flourish when bonds and relationships are built and nurtured. In other words, we must communicate in all its forms to build upon our personal social interaction quotient; allowing one form of interaction can undermine development.

The value that we as humans place on the physical presence of each other is powerful. In Eastern and Western societies, the ultimate punishment for prisoners is solitary confinement. Prisoners have the privilege of being social, of interacting, taken away. Humans are social entities, and our personal growth depends on this, hence the SIQ. Likewise, a form of punishment used by parents is "time out," where the child is displaced from others or the toy, or another artifact she was interacting with. We require the SIQ to build the bond with self and other.

Henceforth, when strong bonds are broken, we become weaker and may lose the ability to empathize. Facebook, Twitter, Instagram and other forms of social media are excellent examples of tech-based social interaction. While we "connect" electronically, these forms of communication have limits. We fail to see gestures, facial expressions, glances, surprises, eye movement or eye contact and body language. All such markers and indicators of interest and emotional play disappear in certain types of tech-exchanges. As we become more dependent on this mode of interaction, we may lose the ability to develop SIQ. Would this be debilitating to empathetic understanding?

Studies have shown that children are entering high school unable to write due to the amount of texting they do. I doubt we will forsake the ability to interact face-to-face, but certainly these indirect modes of relating are diluting our connections and this scenario is one worth thinking about. Most imminently, if we undervalue interfaced connections, how would we articulate self-mastery and how would empathy thrive? We require physical face-to-face communication to develop the sense of self.

The discipline of sociology teaches the various foundations of social interactions. My courses have an enrollment of students from almost every faculty. This is significant because, regardless of the area of study—medical sciences, business, economics, engineering—we

all need an understanding of social interaction processes. In the working world, driven by career mentality and aggression, we must be able to interact and communicate effectively.

To become emotionally intelligent, we require consistency between our inward thoughts and extrinsic actions. The stronger our sense of self, and deeper level of self-mastery, the more empathetic and compassionate our interactions become, people respect our presence, enjoy our company, and feel empowered by our humble sincerity to their well-being, whether it is in a family setting, work environment, or place of leisure. Therefore, to have a high EQ, the prerequisite is self-mastery.

There is only one secret to success, and that is simply to treat others as if we stood in their place—the way you would want them to treat you. We are a product of our interactions, both positive and negative. Our exchanges give rise to our ownership of self. How would we become who we are if it were not for everyone else? Personal connections are action-based. For example, in the corporate world, team mentality is built upon the recognition of the nuances and genuine appreciation of our efforts. Here a forum of similarities and difference can be shared, and this enriches the scope of interactions, elucidating depth. Often, electronic modes of interaction may become one-dimensional.

How Do We Cultivate the SIQ?

The 11 Steps Toward SIQ and Empathetic Understanding

I-N-T-E-R-A-C-T-I-O-N is the acronym for developing the SIQ. Each letter stands for a feature in SIQ development. While certain features are self-explanatory, others I outline below.

- I: Interaction/intellect
- N: Nurture
- T: Train
- E: Emotion/empathy
- R: Rehearse
- A: Attitude
- C: Create/critique
- T: Test
- I: Identify
- O: Opinion/observe
- N: Nuance

Depending on one's *intellect*, level of intelligence, socioeconomic status, educational level, individuals are more or less equipped with knowledge for interacting in *certain* ways with different people. In fact, it is a myth to believe highly intelligent people may be effective communicators. Intelligence does not equate to effective interactional abilities.

That is why the IQ and EQ have unique parameters and different features of validity. Together, they bridge important elements of one's persona in a balanced style. We must also question the face value of assumptions. For example, someone may be shy and yet intelligent, and the other may be highly social yet less intelligent (depending on how we measure and define intelligence).

In taking time and energy to *nurture* yourself, you are better able to nurture others. Women often forget about their needs when consumed by constraints of family and children's needs. We know how important the nurturance of self is; think about the refreshing feelings and clarity of thought that returns when we go on vacation and care for our self. Most importantly, this renewal serves us well and those we care for benefit profoundly. A sense of positivity about self is created when we nurture our spirit. Our relationships strengthen because we are not merely sacrificing the self. Significant to the renewal process and practice of self-mastery, nurturance gives momentum to self-worth for you and the people you interact and associate with.

Training your mind toward acceptance and openness for another's point of view is a difficult task; if it were simple, we would not be having differences, arguments, disagreements with others. Yet this also captures the diversity of human interactions and gives rise to interest. Could you imagine interacting with the same type of personality all the time? We would become bored quite easily. Thus, we need to encourage the self to accept other's uniqueness. A broader state of mind allows for *varied* and inimitable interactions. This builds character and confidence.

179

Openness towards your interactions aids the opportunity to connect with people from various paths in life; this drives self-mastery with depth and deeper associations. We do not see people as one-dimensional, but we recognize complexities and the layers of differences we have. Just imagine how enriching to one's being this can be.

For example, at the dinner table, a friend or relative may ask what kind of day you had. More than likely you relay a story about an interaction that was very positive or very negative. The interaction you chose to speak of would be a highly charged negative or positive interaction. And if nothing significant happened, we relay those mundane interactions. Of course, all communication is significant, but those that touch us deeper on an emotional level are also the ones that affect our spirit.

Self-mastery brings forth awareness to these emotions, both positive and negative; otherwise, they simply remain in the air. We choose to talk about exchanges that are highly charged with emotive qualities, whether these were positive or negative emotions. The choice of what interactions we choose to talk about on a given day also demonstrates the effect on us and the things we value.

Have you ever found that consistently you may talk about daily events around the same person? Perhaps you tell stories of a toxic coworker most evenings at the dinner table. If the same coworker acts in a way, you do not expect you have more drive to discuss an interaction. This is very telling because the person obviously has a profound effect

on your emotions. Conversely, a complete stranger may be your topic of conversation. Perhaps you met someone who acted in an unruly or kind way. You would also speak of this because it made a profound difference to your day.

I recall one Wednesday morning, I was rushing to work; regardless of how late I am, I have a way of convincing myself I do have a minute to spare to drive through Starbucks. This was one of those mornings, and as I got into the lane, I realized there were at least six cars ahead of me. Too late to back out, I was stuck, and all I could think about was that I would be late with four hundred students waiting in a hall. They wouldn't be happy. I take responsibility; they should be upset because I should not be late.

I had no choice but to wait, and finally it was my turn. I ordered a tall coffee and oatmeal cookie. The barista said the car before me gave her ten dollars to pay for my order, and I was silenced. I asked why. She said it was someone who wanted to be kind, by chance because it was "random act of kindness" day. A random act of kindness! I insisted on paying and she said that was not necessary.

As I drove off, I could not believe what had occurred. It was such a kind gesture. And more than the coffee and cookie, I was thinking about the action of the person and how it made me feel we can be kind to each other, if for no reason at all. This was my dinner story that evening, and it was about someone I had an invisible interaction with. All I shared with my husband was the line in the Starbucks drive-thru. As for being late, I entered the lecture theater

with a smile. I told the students my story before beginning the lecture. I even suggested we all perform acts of kindness for the day. They cheered, laughed, and even forgot they had to wait five minutes as I received a kind cup of coffee.

Our *emotion*s are signifiers of how we feel. After a single interaction with another person, we can have a combination of emotions and an intensity of various emotions happening at once. Interactions give rise to the emotional placement of recollecting events in our life. We think about people and events based on *how they made us feel.* Those interactions that invoke feelings of pleasure, satisfaction, and happiness, were connections where the other acted toward us empathetically.

We may not realize this at the time, but those feel-good emotions occur when people relate to us, and that is why we feel positively. Often we may believe we connect with someone because they are "relatable." Relatability is when the other party acts empathically, otherwise we would not be able to sense the association. Our interactions are categorized from the emotions they invoke. As you read this section of the book, think of five events that were significant in your life. Write down one word to describe each event. Are the descriptors of the events emotional descriptors?

The intensity of emotions is a powerful force of action. Feelings can mend or destroy our relationships and even alter the trajectory of our lives. Why are bad moods "contagious?" The effect of the emotion can enlist others to

feel the same; such is the power of our emotions in driving our interactions, and hence the way we invoke empathy for each other. A constantly fearful or angry person cannot act with empathy because they lack self-mastery. Sadly, they ache for attention from others and perhaps act selflessly toward others, rather than giving their attention to their self first.

The more we interact and spend time with our self in solitude, the more we are *rehearsing* self-mastery, and we become better. As with any talent, you gain confidence and courage in your ability with practice. One does not become a great tennis player, musician, scientist, or ballerina overnight. Rehearsal, time, and dedication for years leads us to the mastery of a calling. By practicing self-mastery, we rehearse those attitudes that foster compassion first for self, then others.

When we interact, we share ideas, thoughts about objects, events, aesthetics, medicine, philosophy. Self-mastery is the forum to rehearse and articulate our fears and biases about all these facets of our life, in solitude. We become better at sharing our perspectives with other's unique perspective. A strong self-worth is what allows this to happen. Self-mastery enables cognizance of our own and others' biases. If we interact with a stockbroker who believes strongly in the overall rise of the markets historically, we do not necessarily become easily swayed by his opinions. Rather, by way of self-mastery and a strong sense of self-worth, we have the tools for being self-informed. We are not easily influenced—we can

understand different perspectives. Thus, self-mastery builds our sense of self in that we know what we strongly believe in while allowing others to do the same. This is paramount as it allows us to make informed life decisions, about significant and mundane things in our existence.

Creativity consistency and *compassion* are the side effects of self-mastery. My passion for the creative elements of human existence is found in my words, *creativity is manifest intelligence,* an expression that has been used by many. This is a statement I believe and live by. Self-mastery flows from the creative perception of self we all feel. To perceive, we must create. How does this happen? We may require a nudge to do a new activity, for example taking a cooking or art class, or going to a gym. We then realize we love the activity; in being creative, we come to know our passions.

Creativity connects us deeper to our self and our thoughts. When painting, writing a poem, book, composing a piece of music, the solitude, stillness, silence an artist feels is the motivating force of the artistic endeavor. This is the nucleus of self-mastery and self-interaction. Creating outlets that enliven interactions help to build your personal portfolio of self-based interaction. More important as we create opportunities to meet and interact with others, we need to create such opportunities for our self too. Apart from self-focus, we should try to interact with as many *kinds* of individuals that are unique from our norm. This enhances your interactional web of connections. As we branch out an investment portfolio, diversifying types of

184

interactions only can help to deepen our understanding of self because we draw on unique frames of reference. *Time* is the penultimate driving force of self-mastery. Time is a precious commodity, time is money, but time is also how we nurture our self-worth. We must prioritize by placing time aside for the self, alone time, not a distraction. I refer to this in chapter one; self-time is our most valuable moments. It is what gives rise to our best self, and makes us our best for others.

The practice of self-mastery creates in us an *interest*, passion, and zeal for life. Through self-mastery, we become confident and grounded. We feel we can enjoy life because we routinely work at nurturing our self-worth. With a strong self, we can climb mountains, go into space, and discover cures for diseases. We can make a big and small difference in other's lives because we are steadily granting our self that power.

To forge a life of fulfillment is to be *open* and understanding about the plight and different existence of people who are unique from us. Self-mastery opens the corridor of our minds, to be accepting and treat others well.

Finally, I see self-mastery as a *necessity* for us to thrive and have fruitful interactions. Just as we must care, and provide the basic necessity for our children, we must also begin with the most basic need of our existence—the care for the Self above all else. Self-mastery is the necessity for interactions that are cloaked in kindness.

Chapter Six
The Power of Self-Mastery
Types of Interactional Power

Political power is not exclusive to politicians. In fact, all relationships are power-laced and diplomatically driven. We know even the most sensitive and intimate relationships between partners are power-laden. Often thought of as altruistic in nature, the parent-child relationship is imbued with power. The bond between a mother and child could have political nuances giving rise to self-interest, depending on cultural values. Among many things, a mother uses her knowledge and power of speech to teach her child etiquette. Her self-interest lies in the fact she wants her child to make her proud by having good conduct. She is ingratiated further if the child's manners are recognized by others. Parents give unconditionally to their children, but they also hope the child will become responsible and independent.

Power in and of itself is not an unscrupulous entity; it generates a deleterious connotation because history is flooded with examples of the sordid abuse of power. Conversely, power is used for freedom, to help the less fortunate, to bring awareness to important causes and for economic prosperity. Indeed, power could be a conduit for driving prosperity and productivity in our lives; it is what we do with the power that is essential and significant to its purpose. Ellen DeGeneres, Beyoncé, Julianne Moore, Angelina Jolie, and Emma Watson are solid examples of strong women who have power and influence and use it as

a means for helping others around the world. Julianne has used her power to speak up against cosmetic procedures; Oprah for creating schools for girls to be educated in Africa, among so many other causes; Ellen is a spokesperson for gay rights; Angelina as a United Nations Ambassador; and Emma supports women's literature that celebrates equality and feminine dialogue.

Power of Paying Attention

Self-indicators of power and deciding who has power in our personal interactions are indeed complex. This gradation serves as an important indicator for self-mastery. To exemplify, contemplate the following scenario. When engaged in a conversation, who holds greater power: the individual speaking or the person listening? We may assume it is the person speaking. However, from a different arc, it can be reasoned the one listening has more power because the other person *trusts* you enough to be sharing stories and ideas with you.

As the listener, you can decide how much to divulge of yourself based on the other person's story. You may decide she is not ready to hear your story or simply that the other person is not deserving of your story or trust. Power is about trusting; we trust politicians, lawmakers, our families, educators to act in certain ways to protect our interests. In some cases, we do not overtly question their roles because we imbue them with power for the sake of the role they play in our lives. Further, we all hold power in the most significant and insignificant ways that we may or may not be aware of.

Self-mastery practices will account for feelings of powerlessness. The practice itself empowers us because we build a strong sense of self. Inner power is gained from self-worth. Hence, your feelings of worth offset materialistic driven power you may not feel you have. Gradually, we gain inner strength which becomes our reservoir for feeling personally powerful because we *attribute* this power to our self. Most importantly, we do not crave its excision in our material life, because our inner feelings of value compensate. Those who abuse power believe that others have thrust upon them the right to their power, and therefore because it was given to them, they have a unique right to exploit and abuse it, ultimately displaying their own lack of self-mastery.

The Secret of Winning at the Game of Life
Manifold Effects of Spirit Injury

In North America, we will most likely remain in the same social class as our parents: nostalgia of hopelessness carries forward for generations. We must break the cycle and get off the dilapidated path by aspiring to more.

Insofar as we must change our mindset to believe we can be more, I refer to the practice outlined below:

The Winner effect: In essence, you must think you will win, and you will be a winner. Winning is a conception in our thoughts that must be converted to action for the aspiration of a goal. We all think, dream of winning at

something we are passionate about. Failure to act upon that thought endures it to an existential standstill in our mind.

Instead, thoughts must be placed in disarray, in a state of flux. This is how we contemplate. Thought patterns cannot be static; they must be malleable. Faced with a significant decision, we do not think in a one-dimensional mode about it, rather we look at all aspects and trajectories to come to a final decision. So too, rigorous action is required if we want something and especially if we want it enough. Material possessions can make us happy only transiently, temporarily.

Self-mastery enables the *realization* that obtaining a material possession or object of amour elicits but a passing high; this awareness places us into the realm of emotional maturity.

Therefore, materialistic possessions act as an illicit drug whereby the nirvana only lasts a short time, as with anything on the surface. To feel genuine happiness, we must delve beyond the surface high. Temporary nirvana is a state of grace, bliss, joy, paradise, pleasure, spiritual enlightenment. We all seek temporary nirvana because the permanent state is impossible for most of us to aspire to and such a self-actualization is met by few of us in our lifetime.

To exemplify, the state of monkhood means one gives up all material aspects of life. Since most of us will not aspire to this, we can at least transitorily enjoy moments of happiness in our lives.

As a young mother, spending my days alone with my baby, it was difficult to live every day only caring for my little one. As much as I loved her, I was not interacting with any other human being aside from my husband. In planning a night out to enjoy myself with friends, I knew I also had to return to my work as a mom and the most important elements of my life. Looking forward to time away was a type of temporary nirvana for me. It was indeed a pleasure to know I would not worry about anything except enjoying myself and having fun. These times made me a better person to perform my task-oriented roles. It gave me a sense of purposeful power.

The Elegance of Power for Your Win in the Game of Life

Power can be cloaked in humility and kindness rather than arrogance and conceit. The power in you lies in the far-reaching destiny you assume for yourself. Predetermination is merely limiting. We make choices and create our own path to success and power. Your power is driven by your own self-interest because no one else other than you will have your greatest interest at heart. Historically, those with self-admonishing interests have sold their ideas to the masses swayed by hopes of improving their lives. History has taught us differently. Life is hard work and punctuated by miniscule moments of pleasure and happiness. One requires drive and motivation to keep going. This must be accompanied by effective strategies and ideas.

Sociologist and philosopher Pierre Bourdieu develops the concept of habitus.[xxvi] The habits we set for ourselves, in turn, decipher the kinds of strategies we use to win. "Game playing" improves how well we articulate action required for success. The biggest winners are often those with newly derived and innovative strategies; in other words, those who do not necessarily conform, and of course this could be contentious.

One of the first things parents teach their children is they must not cheat in life, at sports, school activities or academics; cheating is never acceptable. Children are taught to play a game effectively using strategies utilized, shaped, and proven effective over time. In a game of chess, concentration, mental capacity, and memory become of absolute importance.

Additionally, children who master the game-playing process learn perhaps the most important lesson of all: how to lose. Winning becomes secondary because the focus is on the process of strategizing to your best ability. With this knowledge, losing a game is actually winning. Despite a loss, a child may display excellent sportsmanship and genuine appreciation for the winning opponent's talent. Essentially, the loser is able to be defeated in an elegant style, to accept the loss and move forward. This practice enables children to become winners at the game of life, regardless of the outcomes they are faced with.

Power of one: you: Winners have a belief in themselves that to some extent requires a narcissistic shift. While empathy moves away from narcissism—you are

thinking more about the other than yourself—winning does impart some conscious notion of self-absorption. Winning is a state of mind and winners switch it on and off, which can actually manipulate another person's state of mind positively or negatively. This creates a parallel exchange. This is the power of the mindset and it nurtures self-mastery. We may loosely call this mind-reading. To think of yourself as a winner is a captivating mode of thinking. It relies on an array of patterns that emerge in the mind.

Science relies on configurations of patterns repeated in certain ways; in turn, this allows for predicting universal values by means of scientific inquiry. So too, our personality forms by individual patterns that lead to predictability. Winners are in tune to their behaviors and reactions. They readily identify these configurations. Obviously, life is laden with surprises, but the idea here is to recognize the overall silhouette of things in our personal life.

For example, as you enter your place of work with fifty other people on a Monday morning, there are inevitable "normal" conversations that take place. We greet people in one way or another, out of respect or interest. For the sake of small talk, we ask about their weekend and what they did. These are our mundane yet expected normals. Only when something goes wrong do we really become attuned to how much we thrive on these mundane aspects of life. To further exemplify, you may go to work on a Monday morning and find an unexpected disruption or commotion. This becomes the focus of the day's dialogues and

communication amongst people because it was unexpected. Thus, while we have unique lives, personality traits, families, experiences, and emotions, we have and live by a generalized shape of expectations.

Self-mastery facilitates conversations with the self to foresee reactions to various events. Knowing our potential reactionary patterns is a powerful self-mastery tool. One is better prepared to deal with both predictable and unpredictable life events, personal or professional, with a sense of preparedness. We certainly cannot foretell everything in our lives; however, being well prepared by the practice of self-mastery can alleviate agony. Life is laden with unforeseen surprises, but self-mastery generates strength with an inner voice that says we are adept at accepting and being flexible to the circumstances that fall in our paths.

Strength of spirit transfers the human psyche and switches it on to winning. A strong sense of being must be a precondition for a winning state of being. Imagine if you consistently think you are incapable, how will you conduct yourself and your life interactions? For example, you may love the game of tennis. However, you feel that because you often lose tennis matches to a friend, you must be a terrible player. By internalizing "I am not good at tennis," you uphold a negative mentality.

Deleterious thinkers focus on the loss rather than the win. To focus on the win imparts a positive approach even toward what you have lost; self-mastery elicits this. Thinking your opponent won because his serve was better

or he had better positioning can be used to motivate a positive approach to your loss. You may instead ask yourself how you can use those strategies to enlist a winning game for yourself. Thus, you must become innovative to harness your win, *your way*, while remaining respectful to norms. If absolute conformity to strategies of the game was not giving you the outcome you wanted, then think of strategies at once unique and in keeping with the core ideas, only with your twist! This is the strength of spirit and sense of self-dimension that proclaims "you can." In moments of self-mastery, you review in your mind strategies that work, do not work, and may require further development.

By the end of this process, you become a winner through reflection and conscious attitude. You become insightful. Winners themselves may become indolent. To remain at the top, we cannot be complacent. Both winners and the underdog must keep working to maintain a winning position. This requires unswerving hard work. The self-mastery mindset is an assuredly strong, worthy one. We always win through genuine effort, not because we have outdone a competitor.

Contemplation of actions leads to winning at the game of life because we reason our losses, our struggles. Contemplation develops non-conformist strategies. The loser that walks away with a grunt is pitiful because he lacks empathy for not being happy for the other's achievement. He also lacks focus on the self because the anger comes from a lack of development of that strength of

spirit I refer to above. Similarly, a winner who displays arrogance and smirks at the loss of another only reverses their win with such an attitude. Empathy must be displayed in positive and negative situations; this is how it is practiced effectively. We give empathy in dire situations, but we also must give empathy to show we are happy for others and share in their joy.

The Beauty of Personal Interactions

Social media has transformed communication with an astounding force. We can reach many people at once as we send out messages of our personal endeavors and interests. High-ranking celebrities and politicians can get their messages across with a grand force. However, is social media discouraging face-to-face interaction? Would you rather get a text message, Facebook post or Instagram greeting saying "happy birthday," or a handwritten card? When a person takes the time to go to a store, select, read through many cards and choose one for you, write in it then post it, they have imparted their own time and effort. Even if it were a lunch-hour errand, they did it for you. Does it become more meaningful than a text message? Does the effort create meaningfulness? Intuitively, we know this is significant, but we also conform to what everyone else is doing, and this may not always be the most nurturing from an interactional stance. Intuitively, we can decipher if the person is important enough.

Roaring whispers are the conversations and small vignettes we have with our self; it is that inner voice, known as intuition. We have these dialogues daily as we act out our various roles. When we do not take time to practice self-mastery, we fail to articulate the meaningfulness of our instinctive conversations. We must realize these exchanges with our self are imbued with intention. We must own them.

Emotional Injury and Self-Mastery

Across the world, sports—the pride of a nation's Olympic team—are a solid example of how we celebrate outer physical strength and athletic ability. In sports, we see the fruition of physical strength, dedication, and perseverance of amazing athletes. However, their physical manifestation of strength could only have been nurtured by inner strength. The physical strengths are but a mere display of interior strengths and dedication to self-mastery to build that self-worth. Thus, we cannot ignore the importance of the invisible inner strength. It is our *weakness* that gives rise and nurtures our strengths. For athletes, the feeling of weakness that stems from the loss of a competition, or disappointing their nation, family, coach, or community, is a driving force for their agility. Our emotional strength is derived from the adversity and weakest moments of our existence. For high achievers, a loss can promote an ambitious need to win.

Indeed, emotional injury can give rise to empathetic understanding as we heal from negative life experiences. Emotional injury can involve drastically overt experiences or subtle actions. Can you recall subtle experiences that

made you feel insignificant? Sometimes we deem them as trivial and try to bury them because they may elicit too much sensitivity. It may simply be too difficult to deal with and confront a hurtful situation at a particular point in time. Perhaps we were made to feel devalued, and it drove us toward emotional injury. The pain enacts in the outer extremities, manifesting in addiction, depression, mental illness, anxiety, violence, and outbursts. At times we go through life wanting to fix *that* wrong. And if we do not fix them as we move through life, with the contemplation of self-mastery, a number of injurious spirit experiences can confound.

We all have these, but some of us depending on circumstance may have different kinds of injurious experiences making us unaware of our reality. It is those individuals with heightened forms of spiritual injury that require support and intervention alongside self-mastery. We all experience spirit injury, but when it is less extreme, we can heal and help each other by the practice of self-mastery.

Detachment and Attachment

None of us are exempt from emotional injury, no matter who we are; indignant feelings are an intricate part of the human condition, interwoven in our daily lives. How we heal and move forward after emotional injury is one of the most powerful actions for developing self-mastery. In childhood, the template for the way we heal is often set in motion (seeing one's parent drink alcohol to alleviate pain or witnessing parents talk, shout, use drugs, smoke). The ways in which we transcend spiritual injury can heavily direct our lives. This can set the stage for our way of coping for the rest of our lives.

The most powerful amongst us, such as the late Steve Jobs, have drawn our awareness to their struggles. From this, the rest of us realize we are not alone. By relating to prominent individuals' struggles, we appreciate and understand our own shortcomings. It is crucial to share thoughts around hardships because if we do not, they fester and the result is ongoing embedded anger, an anger that disrupts the self-mastery process.

Anger, according to the American Sociological Association, is an under-researched emotion.[xxvii] We all carry inhibition or feel humiliation during or after expressing anger. Sensationalistic news stories and media representations of anger reinforce the pervasive notion that to express anger is to show *loss of control of our self.* When angry we forge insults, sarcastic remarks, we shout the most hurtful things, say words we do not mean out of frustration.

We become guilty of hurting and harming one another emotionally. We feel disgust and contempt because someone we love hurt *us.* In turn, we feel contempt for our self because we lost the battle with our self-control. Anger undermines our ability to cope. On the other hand, happiness and less contentious emotions are heavily researched because we are more willing to talk about these; these are emotions that carry far less social embarrassment.

Amidst Anger and Empathy

Scriptures rarely show displays of anger except in the negative. Anger has historically become synonymous with hostility, and nobody wants to seem hostile. Hostility can, in turn, give rise to aggression, deferring self-mastery. Humans become angry because we feel demeaned. Someone insulted us, threatened, neglected, hurt, disrespected our ego.

Moreover, it is usually those closest to us, the ones we love and respect—family, friends, coworkers, colleagues, acquaintances—who have the influence to anger us inconceivably. Being told you could not do something creates anger and hurt. We can all relate to this; we hear success stories of celebrities, actors, singers being told they "could not" despite their success. Only a handful of people move beyond and acquiesce themselves toward success. Their resilience to garner success was or is ingratiated by being told they could not, did not, have the ability, were not good enough. More of us must pursue this path, and in order for us to do this we must be brave and audacious. Audacity is the bravado to be bold.

Anger can be understood in its relationship to empathy. These are not opposing feelings, but they can productively complement each other. While further research is required in this area, I observe that when we feel hurt, the wound exists because we cannot conceive someone we trust, a spouse or parent, could harm us. How can we turn such anger into empathetic understanding? How can we channel our anger toward becoming empathetic? Resentment leads

199

us to want to shut others out, and we disregard their presence, sometimes in hopes of somehow "getting back" at them or wanting to be alone. Why? We aim to understand *what* annoyed us or *how* the person acted incensed.

Alone time helps us to gain a better understanding of why we feel the way we do. I realize this seems counterintuitive. I am asking you to basically be drawn to and have empathy for those who hurt or upset you, even egregiously. After all, anger drives us away; we walk out, slam doors, slam phones, or even jump out of windows or cars. However, if we are able to channel this anger in a way that tells us something about our self—our anger is giving us a message, not so much about the one who hurt us, but about our self. We feel sad because we love them, we feel threatened or that our trust was broken. Ask yourself, why did the angry situation happen? Perhaps you were not attentive?

Ascertaining our anger rather than forgetting or pushing it away moves us into the realm of what I term as progressive anger, opening our hearts for self-mastery. This is anger with intention, relevance, and purpose. This resolve is not to express bitterness or vehemence, but to turn that bitter frustration into an aid for understanding *you*; in other words, for self-mastery. Thinking about angry experiences promotes awareness for what our triggers are, and while certain experiences are awfully hurtful, it is always better to think of the hurt and cry and express frustration rather than push it into the subconscious. Here I note that certain experiences in life can be intense and sometimes require medical and professional interventions. Self-mastery alongside professional care enables the healing process of angry wounds.

How anger drives success: Dealing with anger is important to our emotional sense of self-worth. We are ashamed to talk about anger; there are many books on joy and happiness because it is easier talk about uplifting emotions. We are afraid and ashamed to speak of our anger. Often, we are told that when angry, displace yourself, take deep breaths, stay calm, deal with it. Our fear in expressing anger lies in our fear of disappointing others. Why? Because expressing our anger in their presence exhibits to them that we lost control. When looking at news stories, oftentimes the most sensationalistic ones are those where celebrities, politicians, or the homeless are overtly displaying anger. We are overwhelmed with images of angry protesters who have war or civil unrest in their country, refugees who are fleeing, striking workers not paid enough, protestors fighting for gay rights, etc. They are exposing a valid vulnerability, and we watch in awe.

But what if we have conversations about anger, that it is okay to express, okay to exhibit? When anger festers, the explosion is usually significant. We cannot deny that we all get angry, and we must embrace the conversations about this misunderstood area of our emotional life. This is a conversation that can enable self-mastery. In addition to being progressive, anger alleviates the loathing we can internalize for others. To hold on to abhorrence for another eventually converts to self-loathing, and this is dangerous. Because awareness disallows our anger to become pervasive, awareness is productive and can change the trajectory of our thoughts. We learn to embrace different pathways. Unexpressed anger coupled with fear can be a dangerous combination if left to itself. Anger fulfillment happens when anger is expressed in the mode of productive anger; we gain anger fulfillment when we can fulfill the tensions of being angry. Hence, we can better empathize.

Anger and Fear

As with empathy, we can further find a dialectical relationship between anger and fear. The danger of fearfulness is it encourages weakness rather than strength. To transcend our fears, we must be strong. If fears control our actions, we give in to weakness. There is a complementary relationship between anger and fear.

Anger leads us to distrust others, and if we cannot share our fears, the result is sadness or depression. Think about the things you fear most—often they are elements of your life you are afraid of losing. The experience of loss creates a path toward depression and affects mental health and well-being. Self-mastery nurtures the tools we need to prepare our minds for dealing effectively with loss and hence fear. We experience anger in all facets of our life, and this pervasive nature of angry emotions could take control of our lives if we cannot recognize the triggers. Self-mastery is the conduit for dealing effectively with anger. As discussed above, we must recognize that anger triggers stem from close relations and other fields of our life, such as education, work, politics, law, community, or cultural institutions.

Those who join a monastery are thought to be self-contained and at a place of peace that expresses comportment and self-mastery. To be successful in this regard, one must channel their anger from purposive to progressive. The transition requires individuals to shed complacency, giving rise to the assertion of inner peace. Once we assert this purpose of inner awareness, we become empowered.

Empowerment is the natural state of being that exists when we gain a mastery of self. Articulating anger productively gives us power. The move from purposive to progressive anger is necessary for our self-growth. To be empowered is no small task or undertaking. We hear the term often, but angry people are not necessarily empowered— they are angry. Those who are empowered are the leaders, professionals who can deal with anger practically. These individuals are in no way better than anyone, but they can move anger from the purposive forum into the progressive realm. In other words, we must move from manifest, overt anger to latent, under-façade anger that *must* be articulated in moments of solitude.

Additionally, self-mastery guides anger toward purposive action. Standing out, those of us who are driven by anger are non-conformist. Anger that motivates change can lead us to aspire further, to be driven. Successful musicians, celebrities, and athletes in our midst readily

share stories about being angry when they were told they did not have "what it takes" to be a success. And this inadvertently drove them. Note that I am referring to a fulfilling personal drive toward goals and achievements; sadly, anger, when not articulated appropriately with measures of self-mastery, could lead to violence and other negative consequences.

Anger can lead us to become audacious and deviate from the norm in pursuit of our goal. Within the confines of cultural norms and values, and while respecting others, individuals who use innovative strategies can soar to greater heights, often leaving most of us behind. They are highly self-mastered because they know their potential and are in potent pursuit of it. The relationship between success and audacity is useful. Anyone who is successful can attest to the fact that success comes with a dimension that we do not often discuss: audacity.

Audaciousness

Subconsciously, we realize and bring the intuitive dialogue to the conscious level during times of self-mastery, we can recognize the messages. For example, you may be having a horrible day; to add to the stress, your boss insults your work. You feel belittled. Perhaps you go over the scenario repeatedly in your mind. You ask yourself, was there a point? Could I have done better? I realize this is very difficult to do because we like to believe we are being disrespected, especially if we complete a project and we *know* we gave much effort. This is where audaciousness can become effective. It takes courage to nicely ask your boss why the work was not to her expectation or why she was exceedingly critical.

With the practice of self-mastery, we gain a deeper level of self-respect that takes us on the path of courage. Those who are not strongly self-mastered are individuals that the boss's comments would fester upon. They may unwittingly try to explain to themselves, to coworkers and the boss, or find reasons and even excuses for why the boss was unsatisfied. This is because they may lack a strong sense of self to confront the situation and ask questions.

On the other hand, the person who questions the boss tactfully, respectfully *knows* her potential, knows her work and *her*self. Therefore, she is not easily discouraged but would take criticism in stride. Often, individuals' disagreeable personalities may have very negative effects on our lives. The power to let others be is easier said than done. We must realize we cannot change the personal attributes of others. We cannot make a spouse more attentive, a coworker less toxic. What we can do is cope.

So rather than try to change others, we must redirect our energies to focus on our behavior. As adults, redirecting yourself is a personal responsibility, and yes, it involves a strong spirit. Self-mastery gives us this spirit. Often we chose to redirect the other person because it is easier than redirecting our self. However, they too must do this for themselves, and that is how we can help others— but at some point, they must be prepared to help themselves.

Using Audacity to Promote Empathy

Audacity or a fearless, bold drive can be attributed to great success. In the context of success, we are often told we must take risks. Such risk taking implies bold audacity. Put another way, nobody realizes success by remaining fearfully complacent. Audacity provides the armor; we hide our fears behind a bold affront. It is important to understand that bold actions should not come at the sacrifice of empathy or awareness of others' premise. Not considering others' feelings is perhaps one of the greatest ills existing in today's world, but greater than that is not practicing self-mastery. Self-mastery is what opens the passage for awareness of self and others. How can this be possible since assertiveness and empathy seem contradictory elements?

As a professor to hundreds of students per semester, I boldly state the objectives of my course and that it is not possible to pass without putting forth time and effort. At the same time, having been a student not too long ago, I understand and sympathize with student angst. It is essential to be bold, to take charge, to provide strong leadership. Leadership is an important factor in acting both boldly and empathetically. The greatest global organizations or corporations—Apple, Google, the United Nations—are led by strong-willed leaders. In most cases, they remain at the helm because their bold, audacious, and empathetic personalities conflate to reinforce effective leadership capabilities. However, while the team leader boldly shares expectations, there is also the feature of the

regressing stance. She is able to step back and permit others to carry out set goals.

The Power of Audacity

Being audacious does not disqualify others. In fact, audacity is at times a purposive means to achieve change. The recent past has shown us that women, marginalized groups, people of color, LGBTQ individuals, and repressive practices against minority cultures could not have aspired change unless people were prepared to act bravely, challenge the status quo and disregard the repressive rules. The suffrage movements, the French Revolution, even the beheading of Marie Antoinette created positive change from audacious behavior. Unless there is a challenge or revolt, how we shall expect change? A main premise of sociological thought is that society undergoes a change depending on the values of a given historical epoch. To expect our society to remain static and regard change as negative is untoward thinking.

Daring to be driven, audacity can, in fact, drive empathy, and herein we find the conundrum. Dominant understanding of audaciousness is that it can be a bold disregard for others. Audacious regard, not disregard, comes about with the practice of self-mastery because our empathy standards strengthen. Let us say that audacious behavior can also be a bold *regard* for others who are repressed, hurt, weak, or vulnerable. When we act audaciously in defense of those practices or groups often marginalized, we act emphatically to create expression and representation for them. To boldly respect the position and will of the suppressed, we act with regard to their needs and not only that of the status quo, and this is compelling.

At the onset, I described how self-mastery gives way to empathy. Further advancement of self-mastery generates the want to help others in addition to helping ourselves. We empathize with those closer to us, and as we gain a stronger sense of self-worth, our empathy flows to other realms. Therefore, self-mastery enables a broadening of our empathy goals. Yes, this thinking implies challenging authority. But if it is for the overall good, the will can be stronger than the challenge.

Sadly, most of us remain complacent out of fear. Fear of losing our position, fear of upsetting norms and dominant values, fear of disappointment. We shy away and then become trapped in the cycles of normality. Therefore, being audacious in the context of self-mastery that I generate here does not mean to hurt or disregard other positions, laws, or bureaucracy; we are bound and must respect law and order. It does mean to act brazenly for giving empathy to the predicament of others. Our actions should aim to change repressive elements of a status quo. Repressive practices in our own household, our place of work, local communities, and globally must be questioned. Self-mastery generates the need for this. The belief in practice does not mean it is correct. Present-day contentious issues such as abortion and capital punishment are such examples.

The audacious person challenges and asserts the belief that a move beyond certain ideas is necessary for everyday existence. It means to subtly apply pressure for change, and this does require bold action. If women were not frowned upon for acting out of the norm, being ridiculed as "hyenas in petticoats," demanding the opportunity to work outside the home, the idea would have remained just that without action. And while the equal pay of men and women is another contentious issue beyond the confines of this book, attention from those who act confidently to alleviate economic inequality begins with challenging the norms of thinking and believing.

To practice audacity, we must master the art of giving consideration to self, thus self-master. Subtle actions can quietly create significant change in contrast to the present decrees of acting audacious. For example, a group of employees may be attempting to have their company allow employees to leave work at 2 p.m. instead of 5 p.m. on Fridays. To suggest this change to your superiors may seem overwhelming. However, if there is a gradual conversation or a specific research citation or article that employees may subtly share with superiors, the idea can be considered.

Anything that initially challenges complacent activities is always seen as impudent, until it becomes a valid or even better alternative to the norm. Audacious thinking is required to attain change. History has many examples of peacemakers who fought for rights of others, and as peaceful as the approaches may have been they were deemed "dangerous" because they questioned repressive practices; for example, Gandhi's actions were thought of as audacious to those in power at that time, although he acted with the practice of peace for all humanity.

The Only Secret to Success
The Clandestine Relationship of Audacity and Self-Mastery

The choice to take the role of other, to not conform, to stand out is powerful. An audacious person is brave, willing to take risks, and driven by courage. Yet at the same time, as I have shown, the audacious person *can and does* act with empathy.

A life of empathy requires mindfulness, living in the present, and knowing how your actions in the present will affect your goals as well as others. There is a method to the madness of thinking before you speak. Why? What you say and do now will affect your future success and experiences. Ruminating on the past will not allow for empathetic understanding because when one persistently ponders the past, she carries the angst of those negative experiences and it becomes all consuming. While past pain is difficult to release, with the practice of self-mastery we do not dwell on the past and look beyond to the future. This notion finds manifestation in our present reality as we move forward. For example, perhaps you receive an award of recognition for volunteer work; put yourself in the space of those who awarded you and recognized your worth. Would they not want to see you do more? If you simply remain complacent with an achievement, you eventually come to lack further

progress. Given health and balance in our lives, we should always want to challenge ourselves further. By remaining complacent, we can regress in goals and negative experiences.

How the regression stance works: This is the point where empathetic understanding becomes a strong entity in interactions. By regressing at the point of successful attainment of a goal, a person tells others, "I have made it." I want to make myself better by empowering you and allowing you to make it too. We commonly refer to these individuals as mentors or those we look up to. Self-mastery gives us the ability to understand our success should give us the drive to feel bold, audacious, and fearless, to forge ahead.

Most importantly, once successful, we must want to help others. Do not confuse regression with giving up. To regress is not to give up at doing better and achieving more. Rather, the stance of regression inspires those of us who are evidently successful at an art, or have a greater talent to *share* this knowledge and talent. In moving ahead to further our goals, this is paramount. A singer who continues to put out great songs, or an athlete that continues toward success, shares their win and becomes a spokesperson for a particular sport. They take pride and share their knowledge and talent with others. The cycle of progress and sharing of talent is a collective effect of self-mastery.

Thus, after the aggressive pursuit of a goal and its realization, the individual must also share that knowledge with others. After all, if one is where they hope to be, at the

top of their game, why stop? Forging ahead seems to be the obvious option but can also give rise to self-absorption, and this is not the same as self-mastery. This is where modernity has failed. Assertive goal attainment is valued in our society. However, having aspired goals when there is no sharing of one's talent contributes to the rise of arrogant me-first ideologies. Egotistical emotions and sentiments create a lack of awareness and empathy for others. Individuals become self-absorbed to the point of self-destructive actions. Self-absorption manifests in mental and emotional problems. From the successful CEO, the greatest sports star, an accomplished artist or scientist, our world has unfortunately borne witness to those who have fallen into addictive behavior after immense success. Success and drive without taking time to contemplate and practice self-mastery leads to surface-oriented, self-absorbed, and addictive behavior.

Addiction imparts both societal and biological attributes. It can be a form of escape for those having difficulty in coping. This results in a lack of want to be present, and substances alleviate pain. In other words, the need to escape from the pain of reality becomes intense. We all know what it is to feel desperate, unable to cope. Addiction thrives when escapism enables the loss of ability to empathize even with the self. This becomes self-destructive. Self-mastery cannot take the place of professional and medical intervention for addiction, but it can propel an understanding of one's needs that goes

beyond the surface. Self-mastery validates the self first and then becomes the conduit for empathy.

I stand as you: For those who by definition are self-absorbed, this is not a crime because our society celebrates and applauds narcissism; we are all a part of this dynamic. For actions of narcissism to be complete, we *require* the role of other. The narcissist needs others to validate his self-centrality whereas self-mastered individuals do not have such requirements. In fact, they seek to validate others. Narcissists can only act out self-immersion in the presence of the other. They need others to feel good about their self. For example, feeling good in an outfit is not enough, the narcissist must post it for others to validate and "like." Additionally, I argue that the more difficult the goal, the stronger the drive must be. When such a drive becomes destructive and selfish is when we begin to tread upon dangerous territory. Narcissists escape society by their actions, but they significantly attempt to escape the self. Ultimately, we find a lack of empathetic understanding for the self, and this reinforces emotionally destructive behavior to self and others.

Ironically, this is also the core of empathetic understanding; we need others to validate us to motivate our acts of empathy. Every individual who validates another *expects* substantiation in return—think of this on a continuum, from high to low validation. This is not an overt or toxic expectation. However, for the narcissist, this validation is always received but never returned. They do not see beyond the validation of self for self, or validation

of self from others. Further, self-validation is limited because we are bound by what family, friends, and colleagues think of us. The common thinking is that we should not care what others think, and I absolutely share this sentiment. The problem is that we *cannot help but care*. We are invested in what others think, we want acceptance. The most common click button on any social media is the "like" button. We know the feelings of likability when others accept what we share. We also know the feeling of disappointment when they do not.

Want for acceptance is part of our nature. Therefore, rather than denying that we care, we must celebrate our talents and validate others uniqueness too. By validating *them*, we show that we accept them. We empathize with who they are and how they are. The message is "I *expect* the same in return." The narcissist fails here.

It is a mistake to assume that we can ignore what others' think—we just cannot. Some of us may be better at ignoring hurtful remarks and actions. Because we know what it is to have hurt feelings, empathy creates this awareness of not acting with harm toward each other, and this is the power of empathetic understanding: kindness begets kindness. Self-mastery is the passageway or the bridge between kindness to self and kindness to other.

Self-Mastery = Kindness to Self + Kindness to Others

It is important to celebrate every achievement. We focus on the big picture, which provides a vision of the

goal, but the attainment of small steps on the path to self-mastery and empathy is important too. The power to achieve anything we want using specific tools is essential. Think of cooking—one would not use a mandolin slicer to beat an egg, one requires an egg beater. Thus, depending on the situation, different types of empathetic tools must also be utilized, from empathy that is re-enacted audaciously to subtler forms of empathy.

Self-mastery drives our understanding to nurture the tools we already possess; those tools become our strengths and guide our weaknesses. Empathetic understanding and having a strong drive, such as being audacious that I discuss above, cannot be confused with aggression. Heightened awareness to get what you want for *your*self is not aggression or self-consuming behavior. It is an assertion that you hold your interests at heart, and dearly so. You have self-respect. Think about this: If you do not have a robust drive for yourself to achieve a goal, who will? Ultimately, this flows over to others in your life and is a beautiful use of our humanity.

The Ingenuity of Self-Mastery and Audacity

Real and fake understanding: We live in a world of pretense. Today, authenticity and replicability have collided. We see imitations of people and objects all around us; it is increasingly difficult to differentiate what is real and what is not. In the same way objects can be created to mislead, our actions can lack faithfulness to the self. This is counterproductive. Self-mastery brings awareness we need to express our genuine self for others to see and appreciate. Those in your life must respect the real you; this is where self-mastery leads to self-acceptance. You are happy about you.

One lively and bright Sunday morning, I sat looking on as the shadows of the green leaves from the trees swayed against the white marble of the kitchen island. My forearms resting on the smooth, cold, and still surface, I stared intensely at the natural grains of stains in the age-old Tuscan marble. Distracted by the swaying obscurities, I scrolled through my Twitter feeds. The top trend was International Day of Happiness. I could see a myriad of depictions of happiness and fulfillment as posted by people everywhere in the world. Happiness was depicted by cuddling with a pet, kissing a penguin, huddling with friends, societies partying, couples strolling with a child, children laughing as they play, pride for a great sports team, appreciation of a best friend, stories of love at first sight, exercising and eating well. The images were truly lovely depictions of happiness by every stretch of the imagination.

This was beautiful yet muffled to me. What I noticed was every depiction of happiness was with persons, objects, or other materials that *made* people happy. Despite my desperate search, I could not find a story of happiness in solitude, of happiness being found with the self. I knew this must exist, I was just missing it. I was made to ponder. It is not the individual's fault we have been socialized to believe we require other things, other people, and other sources to make us happy; after all, we are a materialistic society, and we are all a part of the capitalistic trundle. This message resonates and repeats pervasively.

Every day, we need and require other people and other things to have a sense of self and inner strength. This is disparaging. Self-mastery is the path toward happiness, thus it is necessary to rethink how we look at the constitution of happiness.

Our families, children, friends make us happy; our favorite sweater makes us happy. We have many individuals and objects that transcend delight upon us. However, we ultimately need only one thing to create fulfillment: the relationship we have and share with our self.

If we cannot seek out moments of solitude and practice self-mastery, we cannot feel fulfillment. I express this from the point of view of my many roles.

Happiness Has No Reason

Being a mother, I believed my children were the *only* thing I needed and ever would need to be happy. One day as I watched my children play at the park, I had a thunderous realization. I looked on as they were swinging into the sky, their screams of laughter music to my ears. They seesawed against the streaming water flowing down the curving creek beside us. Simply listening to the humor of their little conversations and arguments with each other should make any mother utterly happy. I was not happy. Should I not be? Resembling everyone else, should I not be

joyful—my children are all I need to be happy, is that not what good mothers believe? What was amiss about these feelings? Yes, my children, my family, my profession made me happy, but they could not make my *Self* happy. Only *I* had the power to do that. With all the wondrous elements of my life, I had no reason to feel hollow. Searching for a *reason* to be happy was my gravest mistake.

To search for your reason of happiness is to believe you need a reason, purpose, and cause. The causation will create only the *illusion* of fulfillment, and most importantly it is *other than you*. We cannot obtain self-mastery while reasoning and negotiating for it. This implies a conscious, material exchange. This is not self-mastery.

You Are

Attempts to reason your self-worth are to place it in the extrinsic world, endowing it with avaricious and worldly significance. *Self-worth is non-negotiable*. However, we fail to realize that self-mastery offers us this awareness. Historically, we have been taught to *understand* and rationalize our sense of self; to find a reason for our happiness. Self-mastery retreats reasoning to simply the state of knowing you are worthy. It is from this sense of self-worth that happiness flows and flourishes. There is *no such thing as searching for happiness. Happiness is not a thing we seek out. It is a state of being derived from self-mastery*. We should have no purpose to seek it, why should there be a purpose? Simply, it is the consequence of self-mastery, being at peace, fulfilled with self.

The search for understanding is second nature to human existence. Whether we are rich or poor, we want a sense of fulfillment; it is a sensation that lies in our subconscious ready to ascend. The intuitive force of self-fulfilling thoughts is powerful. This perception generates the underlying notion that we are the creators of our sense of self. It does not require us to look outward to family, objects, or events to create gratification.

Once we are aware that harmony from within is our greatest accomplishment, her triumphs are merely embellishments. We are aptly able to feel content in any given environment, amongst anyone. Too often, we express outwardly what we are grateful *for*. However, when we encase gratuitous notions to the realm objects—things/persons we are thankful *for* or things we have—we offset the inspirational power of fulfillment. We need to be thankful for being. This demystifies the objective notion of gratitude. Self-mastery elucidates thankfulness for being, not for things.

And in being we appreciate how other facets of our lives (things) come to be. The importance of this is we foster self-awareness first, and things are an indirect result of the sense of self we attain. The shift moves *from self to things rather than things to self*. We are thankful for being in health, being in happiness, being in peace, being in satisfaction. We no longer look upon fulfillment as an object creating this fulfillment, but the object is the *result* of the fulfillment. It is our state of being derived from self-mastery that gives rise to all other sources of satisfaction.

To be is to understand that nothing more than self-mastery is required or expected of *being*. Just simply be.

Echoes of you:

I paused, I pondered, and a heaviness befell me.

–Renu Persaud

The Art of Empathy

When viewing a piece of art, the first element of conceiving is the subconscious emotion. The feeling we get when looking at the work. Some works are so effective at capturing certain emotions of anger, pain, happiness, elation, sexuality that we feel immersed, entangled with the image. For example, thinking about how I related to a van Gogh image, I felt the pain of the artist as he drew the scene, the angst in the strokes, the yellowness of depression. Immersed in a Salvador Dalí work, I imagine his hostility with time as he captured the "warping" of time with melting pocket watches and timepieces. I imagine time as we know it, its divisions into seconds, minutes, hours, days, weeks, months, years, decades, centuries— epochs and light years are but a human construct for manageability of our existence.

Time is our master, enchaining us to doing rather than being. Our personal inner expressions of these artist's feelings allow us to empathize with their reality as they produced the images. So many centuries ago, cave paintings, pain of a discovered mummy, we see the pain on the human's face depicting how the end came by a possible natural disaster. We come to empathize and gain a sense of awe. This process of empathy allows us to connect with these artists and people although they do not exist in our physical environment. This is the art of empathy; we are able to feel for the other, regardless of if they share our physical plain or are physically apart from us.

Artistic Impressions

My love for all artistic forms is deep. Through art we teach, articulate, and transform ourselves in empathy. How can we use self-absorbed behavior from the pursuit of art to help others? One line of reasoning is simply to practice the art of letting others be: by letting others be, you can see your own fire ignite. How do we do this and what are the challenges to being? Further, can those who harbor a broken spirit have empathetic understanding for others? Recall I discussed empathy as fulfilling a fundamental human need we seek that others should *understand* us. A part of this process is that you must first understand yourself. Through tragic events such death of a loved one or tumultuous times of illness, divorce, living through natural disasters, our resilience is tested, and individuals come to have shattered spirits. Can your broken spirit find it in you to feel for others? A mother must be healthy and care for herself first before she cares for her baby. In a similar vein, when you have a broken spirit and you help others, *this process of helping others enables healing in you.* By reaching out, we feel a sense of fulfillment, and it detracts our thoughts to a place of positivity.

Weakness Creates Strength

Everyone around us has a special spark and quality, and we need to celebrate these abilities. I believe it is actually our weaknesses that give rise to our strengths. This is the ultimate paradox, but allow me to explain. Think of your greatest doubts, your weaknesses. You may be afraid of heights, snakes, and other things. In psychology, the use of desensitization therapy is well known. It is meant to gradually alleviate fear. Individuals are steadily desensitized to their greatest fears by embracing and becoming a part of the fearful situation. In confronting the situation you dread, you do not hope it away. Your self becomes a part of the process. If you are envious of the car someone else has, this is a weakness—the act of being envious. However, if you were to befriend that person, learn from them and emulate their success, that element of envy could give rise to a strength you never knew you had.

More than ever, in today's capitalist marketplace, companies thrive and brand themselves as the best in the business. Corporations grow by having the best customer service, best employees, best executives, and best consumer goods. We are a planet obsessed with bests, and there is no question you must be the best to set yourself apart, far apart. To do this, you must first believe you *are*, but this becomes your best-kept secret. Knowing and thinking you *are* the best occurs when we practice self-mastery. This is what I mean by roaring whispers. The silent moments taken to solidify the self itself qualify your position. Certainly,

we must express who we are and what we are, but doing so while being humble is a powerful combination.

People who are the best already know they are from having a strong sense of self-worth. Their power lies in silence. When you have this power, it becomes a talent utilized to your advantage for the benefit of others.

To know in silence you are the best is empowering; most of us should use such power to empower others. This is when you provide empathetic understanding, where you place yourself in another's position. You know what it is to thrive, to try and to fail. Therefore, when you attain success, you must understand you were in the other's position at one time, and encourage and empower others using your silent roars. At this point, when we are able to silently know what it is to be best, we are also able to empower others.

The Compassion Manifesto

The art of mastering you is actually quite simple: Be and let others be too. Aggression and coercion have the opposite effect. Imagine a night without stars; stars are those nuggets of brightness in a life filled with platitudes of darkness.

Life is this way.

It is merely a struggle punctuated by slivers of light and happiness. Self-mastery allows us to whisper loudly and enjoy with pure pleasure our moments of bliss while appreciating that adversity is important to our existence. Self-mastery carries us through a splintered journey toward material bliss. Virtuosity happens when we become talented in the use of empathy as an empowerment tool for parenting, leadership, marketing, personal fulfillment. Dedicating your life to your vocation, endlessly tending to the practical outcome, is merely wasted energy if we do not foster our inner self-worth.

We think of rising up to our challenge as doing something great. But if only we treat people according to the isometrics of self-mastery, we *will* achieve greatness grander than we have ever expected. By greatness here I mean we attain a sense of importance from small or big actions, and this is the rudimentary economics of supply and demand! There are far more of us who do not nurture the greatness of others and only a few of us who do. The irony is to start with yourself, and act selfishly first. Self-aggrandizement is at best used to establish self-worth, to uplift the lives and existence of others. You will stand out and gain admiration for being genuine.

Chapter Seven
The Self-Mastered Artist

A deft Loneliness

My lonely soul, all delight in circles and bonds of friendships, I am left alone

I do not understand the folly of this fragmented existence.

Adroit in ambivalence, this loneliness keeps me asleep, disturbs me in wake, dissolves me in pain, taunts me in anguish,

Loosened silence thin as thread, flow to a place of dread. Never to retain a loyal glory. Disappear in the delight of separation, merely bonded by briars.

A trust always given, never returned. Loneliness is the identity, a defined existence.

Never to belong.

Suspicious eyes hate.

Despair not.

Threats of splendor, concealed in lamb's wool,

Threats of intellect, peace pervades.

In the previous chapters, I demonstrated how you can become the best you by mastering you, for yourself first (and then for the benefit of others.) We all strive to be authorities in our chosen profession, a favorite hobby, parenting, and so on. How often do we think about becoming the best "me"? Energy is espoused in the mastering of various activities in daily life, from making the perfect cup of cappuccino to finding the fastest route to work. In our complex modern-day social life, we forget to focus on becoming experts of ourselves. The value of this premise is clear, as I have reiterated: when you are the best you for you, you become the best you for others! In this way, we can uplift all of humanity and capture the sentiment that we must be better for ourselves first, and this will in turn always extend to others.

The domino effect of niceness may ignite a fire for good reason. This is not meant to be a selfish undertaking by any measure. In fact, it presides in the locus of empathy. If we are able to empathize with ourselves, then we are better prepared to empathize with others.

Think about if it is fair to give those we love, those closest to us, anything less than our full, best self? If we are not self-mastered, we are not only being unfair to our being but to others as well. If we do not take the time and practice self-mastery, we are giving others less of us than they deserve. Surely, your child, spouse, and parents deserve better.

Practices That Enliven Self-Mastery

How do we self-master? In the preceding sections, I offered explanations for why self-mastery is the only path toward a rich and balanced life, connection with your spirit, and nurturing self-worth. The nurturance leaves the effects we can witness in our relationships. We grow in the process and empower others to achieve the same.

Self-knowledge will translate to more effective interactions. When we know how we feel, what our triggers are, we can better interact with others more effectively. Thus, each and every interaction will be maximized.

The Art of Self-Mastery

Self-mastery is the most important aspect of human existence, just as one masters the skill of singing, painting, reading, writing, driving, dancing, and studying, so too we need to master the skill of being our self. Our desire for self-importance and arrogance shows a lack of empathy for one another and results when self-mastery is not nurtured.

As an artist looks upon her beckoning empty canvas, so too we are born tabula rasa, an empty vessel. The artist's action, how they rub the canvas, the lightness, heaviness of brush strokes, depth of hand gestures, will impress upon the canvas the emotions and state of mind of the artist. The nuanced scratches, lines, curves, colors all tell a story. Van Gogh, Modigliani, Picasso, Renoir, Dalí, Kahlo, Cézanne, Farshchian, Degas, Klimt, and many others are artists who exemplify elements of their life coming across in their art. In extending the metaphor to our daily existence, we must seek to know our self. In this knowledge, we find the ultimate art form.

As an artist's vocation evolves with every work, so too we evolve as we work toward self-mastery. We become conscious of our transition toward maturity. Then the point of this is maturity in self-mastery giving rise to empathy. We will all practice self-mastery at different rates because we are unique. The greater we self-master, the more naturally our interactions emanate with consideration.

227

Indeed, it becomes easier to take the role of the other. Our maturity moves from simple to complex. It takes on an aesthetic purpose.

Compassion

Self-mastery is the highest of all art forms. There is nothing more meaningful than knowing yourself, who you are, what you are. Today, overt displays of who we think we are pervade via the Internet, social media, etc. But behind that façade, there is an emptiness that prevails, and while we may not all experience this, many of us do. Added to this emptiness is the violence and destruction amongst humanity. Civil unrest and a deep lack of understanding are pervasive the world over. The public persona takes precedence and the inner self, where self-mastery takes place, becomes secondary, and this is dangerous to our human condition.

Many social ills of today arguably find roots in individuals lacking a sense of self-worth. I believe this is due to a lack of instilling the importance of self-mastery in the global landscape. Self-mastery provides the template, the guide to a balanced life. We all have talents in math, science, and art, but we require the self-mastery template to tease out these talents because if we pursue our talents without mastery of the self, the talent is conceived in hollowness.

Artful Masters

The greatest artists—Monet, Picasso, Klimt, da Vinci—are referred to as masters. Their craft lies in their genius, abilities that are not duplicable. Why do we call them masters? The mastery of their craft did not happen overnight. It was nurtured, given attention. At times the attention and uncertainty must have been discerning, tormenting, not knowing what would happen next. Yet they nurtured their potential. Perseverance led to success. Similarly, we do not know where our practices of self-mastery will find us. Our only constant of existence is uncertainty. We can move beyond this with attention to our inner self. To practice self-mastery and nurture the self from within, one is poised to accept and deal with moments of uncertainty, discouragement, sadness, and disappointment in our lives. More often, we face disappointment, which is why we must value the moments of happiness; for many, these are few. With self-mastery, we better appreciate these moments of pleasure, but more importantly, we create an inner strength that can transcend adversity effectively.

Not coping well could be an effect of lacking self-mastery. Where individuals turn to alcohol, drugs, or abuse are points of departure in losing a connection with our self and inner being. We no longer confront our problems with strength and assertion. We seek to compress our grief into other sources. We create a destructive path, where we slowly walk farther from our sentient being. To regain the strength for self-mastery becomes difficult and at times impossible.

Self-Mastery and the Happiness Threshold

What is true happiness, and how does self-mastery relate to it? One can increase their odds of living a life of optimal happiness by self-mastery because of feelings of fulfillment. At the heart of happiness lies understanding and connection. When we understand something, we enjoy doing it, and when we like someone, we enjoy interacting with them because we feel a connection. But how can we connect with others if we do not connect with our inner self?

To feel angst is to lack an understanding of a phenomenon—we lack knowledge of it, there exists mystery and intrigue of the unknown. By not taking the time to know our self, we live in the mystery of not knowing our true being.

We fear that, because of the unknown, humans would rather know than not. To quell and alleviate fear, we attempt to learn about the matter, object, or person. If we do not understand others, we cannot empathize and we may reject others out of fear. Similarly, if we do not understand ourselves, we lack self-empathy and our fears preside over our own self. In failing to address self, and therefore fears, we become apathetic to our being and existence. To self-master, we address our fears and this opens our minds. Often we reject others out of fear. I argue we also reject ourselves when we do not address our own intimate fears.

230

Ultimately, I summarize this point thus: *How can I love you if I do not love myself?*

We speak of love, happiness, and cherishing those we care about. How can we effectively do this if we do not love our self? Self-mastery is not about self-love. It is about self-worth. To feel you are a worthy human being is the greatest accomplishment and gift you can give yourself. Too many of us feel less than worthy. Society confounds various pressures upon our existence. Competition and ego-driven achievements undermine the things that truly matter.

Thus, self-mastery is also about balance. One may argue a mother can love her child more than herself, and yes, of course this is possible; I have fallen into this trap. However, what is the outcome of this kind of *selfless* love? Ultimately, deep sacrifice leads to unhappiness, and that is why so many women experience depression as new mothers—they feel they need to sacrifice everything to meet the needs of their newborn and family commitments.

On the other hand, research ref shows mothers who have support and retain a connection to the self are better able to adjust to the new reality. This is because they do not leave themselves completely. In retaining a love for themselves, they can become better mothers for their children and family. To love our child, our spouse, our family *effectively*, we must first love our self. We need to cherish and know we are worthwhile.

Self-mastery gives rise to and affects self-worth. When others see that you feel yourself to be worthy, they will treat you similarly. Time and time again we find that individuals who are abused have a history of low self-worthiness when they seek professional help. Often the tolerance of years of abuse confounds by having a low self-esteem. When violators sense you do not feel worthy, they further act to perpetuate this unworthiness.

Buying a car is a simple example that many of us in modern society can relate to. How much time do we put into deciding on the make, model, and color, looking at magazines and discussing the decision? We spend time setting up financing and communicating with the dealers. Could you imagine if you were as meticulous with understanding and learning about all the special and unique facets of you in this way? Mastery of you distills the appreciation of your worthiness. You are healthfully giving of yourself and to others, by paying attention to you first. Do your children, family, and others in your life not deserve this? The movement of society and especially women empowering themselves so they are better parents is nothing new. However, the notion women should be self-sacrificing for their families is a global phenomenon, and women are deemed inferior in the public spheres of work, economics, culture, politics, and religion due to this type of mindset, and this must change.

The domination of so few over so many is a present-day example of how self-mastery lags behind in the human condition. We act according to the design of others because we feel incompetent and lack the confidence to attain personal feelings of greatness. Greatness can only come about with self-mastery. At the same time, our lack of self-mastery disenables us to feel and empathize with the conditions of others.

Willful Neglect of Self

Stress is heightened and stressful situations gain momentum if we do not understand something we are faced with, including our self. Think about one's first week on a new job; whether you are a clerk or CEO of a multinational corporation, we all must adjust and learn about a new position. A few weeks later, we are settled into a routine. Then we attempt to improve our performance to impress our boss or motivate ourselves further. In a like manner, when we begin the process of self-mastery, it may feel odd, especially if we are accustomed to giving to everyone unconditionally. After all, paying attention to you when you are not used to it could feel strange.

Nonetheless, as we notice improvement in our lives that directly correlates to self-mastery, we become hopeful. Eventually, we become dependent on these moments and look forward to them. We nurture our self routinely, it feels good, and we attempt to further improve our performance in various directions of our life.

My friend painstakingly made the decision to attend a Pilates class on Wednesday nights, and while it was initially difficult to leave her new child, a month later she was excitedly looking forward to it. She felt rejuvenated to get back to mothering effectively. She then added an after-class coffee session with friends; it made her feel empowered to share ideas on being a new mother with girlfriends. She was practicing self-mastery by focusing on herself, and in the process, many relationships were being touched by the one positive action. The failure to self-master is that we are overcome with stress and unhappiness. Disillusionment wins. *I refer to this as willful neglect of self.*

Nurturance of your inner eminence preserves the meaning of your life. Today, meaning is lost due to the lack of connection and isolation from our self. Lack of connection means we cannot cope effectively with stress. Thus, how can we be happy and fulfilled, if we do not know how to? While most may agree that we have a good idea of who we are, we do not make time to delve deeper. It is normal for us to use the phrase "getting to know each other" in a dating, working, and friendship context. Have we gotten to know ourselves as responsibly as we should? The semblance of self-mastery takes time and cannot be rushed; it is a gradual process. Further, mastery of self is not a fragmented undertaking. There is continuity, fluidity.

Along with the fluidity of action and depending on our constitution, personal circumstances more or less also affect self-mastery. Therefore, certain experiences that carry highly emotional qualities, whether positive or negative, can deeply nurture self-mastery. The point is to be *aware* and conscious of those moments and use the opportunity to self-master. Often, it is these moments that are ignored when we are overcome with unhappiness or joy.

At times, we want to flee or scream, and our anger, sadness, or disappointment gets the better of us. I realize life is filled with many experiences on a daily basis. Collectively, our experiences create the being we exist *as*. However, being conscious and *aware* of those moments of intense happiness, or intense disappointment, are the times that self-mastery will be most effective in its development. How do we do this? If one is waiting for a phone call about a dream job, the disappointment of not being the successful candidate can be overwhelming, even depressing.

We may seclude ourselves crying while being very angry and frustrated. Some of us may turn to drugs or alcohol, or go out and party to quell disappointment. We do this is to help in hopes of helping ourselves, as we often say "to forget" about what happened. We use such phrases as "this will take your mind off it." We are choosing to forget and deny rather than become self-aware that these moments of sadness or happiness are the moments we should not be forgetting and ignoring.

We should be facing and owning up to the present moment, situate ourselves within our feelings, and contemplate what we have come to know of ourselves for ourselves by this experience. This is self-mastery. This is not to say that one self-isolates. I realize in times of adversity, even a few moments with a close friend or confidant can help us to get through difficulties. We all need such support systems. However, these support mechanisms and relationships should follow those moments of self-mastery, not precede them. By taking this time to self-master, we internalize and comprehend the positive or negative experiences first for us before we draw others into the equation.

In the midst of writing this book, I attended a party where a friend of mine came to know that her ex-fiancé was also at the party with his new fiancé. My friend was devastated. She went into a quiet room of the house, with hopes that nobody would notice that she was missing, overwhelmed with tears. A few friends, myself included, approached her continually to ask how we might help. She replied, "I am devastated, I want to be alone."

I had a life-altering lightbulb moment. I realized this was precisely what I was writing about. Kate wanted to be alone and process the moment, process the experience, and being left alone to do this was her opportunity for self-mastery. Her coping mechanism was crying and isolation; she did not want to be around others at the party. She sat alone for more than an hour.

Left alone, she managed the experience, the complexity of not only being surprised at seeing someone she cared for but also that he was engaged so soon after he broke up with her. In the hour Kate was alone, she thoughtfully created scenarios of "what ifs" in her mind. Perhaps she was disappointed it was not her, perhaps she was angry that he moved on, perhaps she was hurt he did it so quickly, perhaps she was frustrated at feeling "not good enough." The complexities of the situation are far-reaching. However, that hour Kate spent by herself in the drawing room on an ox-blood leather couch, contemplating and dealing with many emotions confronting her all at once, was a valuable moment of self-mastery.

We can learn deeply about ourselves in quiet moments. We need to realize and prepare ourselves to be conscious of *these* moments that propel self-mastery. We will become stronger and secure. This does not come naturally, we must work at it. As humans we are reactionary, and this requires retraining ourselves in moments of despair. While her friends wanted to console Kate, she wanted us to let her be. And this was powerful. In other instances, we may posit that an individual is so distressed, depressed, they should not be left in solitude. Individual emotional and mental health and circumstance must always be given consideration. Therefore, we must judge the situation we are in appropriately. At times, facing a situation or pushing oneself right into it can also be opportunities for self-mastery, and of course we must decide what is best for us.

On the snowy, hazy Christmas evening of 2015, my neighbor left to pick up desserts to bring back home for the festivities. Driving east on his way back, he saw a young girl crossing the road with a bag. He was driving in the westbound lanes. It was dark, and the area was not well lighted except for a dim iron lamp post. He saw a young girl, about eighteen, get struck by a taxicab. Although he was driving in the opposite direction going east, he made the sudden decision to turn the car around and return to the scene.

The girl had fallen on her stomach, face flat on the shiny-iced road. She was bleeding profusely. At that point, my neighbor called 911. He attended to the young girl and noticed she was trying to be strong, but English was not her first language. The cab driver who struck her was shaken, concerned, and nervous. They waited impatiently and in disbelief for help to arrive. My neighbor later described feeling empathy for the young girl; her bag went flying, and it had a newly packaged curling iron in it that she had obviously just bought. Now in a split moment, her entire life had changed. The ambulance arrived, statements were taken. He noticed pearly white beaded objects where the girl fell, and realized they were her teeth. Having a medical background, he collected them and gave them to the ambulance driver for re-implantation.

The example provides many lessons for self-mastery. First, an individual who helps a complete stranger has taken time to *selfishly* practice self-mastery. His act is not mitigated in any way. But his decision to act in such a way is the effect of a stronger sense of self. This gave rise to the compassion and need to help a stranger.

Continuity of the practice of self-mastery is important because it is developing process. As the example above shows, we nurture self-mastery within the experiences that we have. Secondly, in helping the young girl, he not only saved a life, but he gave her hope. Were his actions selfish?

Admirably, we can argue yes, because in helping her, he made himself feel worthy, feel good. However, I do not think this is what motivated him. In helping her, he further attained a deeper level of self-mastery because he acted with empathy. He placed himself in another's position, he

felt her plight. He made a conscious albeit quick decision to help, he knew his actions could help, and he did not hesitate to thrust himself into the situation. To achieve this, he did not isolate himself as Kate did in a previous example, but being in the present, being conscious in the moment, gave rise to the decision. Self-mastery is this consciousness, we can put our self into a situation or displace our self away from a situation, we choose what is best for us. Depending on the conditions, self-mastery can take place in the midst of or in isolation of these moments.

We must have a conscious awareness, because we use these moments to our advantage for nurturing an understanding of our self. Hearing my neighbor recount the story and the myriad sentiment, passion, and feeling compelled him toward a deeper level of self-mastery. How do I know this? Because as he spoke of the experience, he commented on how he felt, what he learned, what he thought. *He empathized, and such empathy is the compelling contrivance of self-mastery.* Acting to help others, even strangers, we are self-mastering that which is the most important human vocation: our ability to take the role of the other, our ability to feel their pain, our ability to sense their fear. However, as I have reinforced all along, we cannot do this unless we are nurturing ourselves toward self-mastery *first*.

Evolution of Self

Self-mastery is an evolving vocation, and material circumstance certainly affects our ability for self-mastery.

Living in wealth or existing in poverty does not mean one cannot self-master. Material existence of any kind is what gives rise to self-mastery. Happiness is elusive, thus being rich does not guarantee happiness nor does it guarantee we are poised toward self-mastery. Similarly, being poor does not exclude one from being able to self-master. Rather, our state of mind and the mindset we have is paramount. How can we be happy without the knowledge of self?

Do you *know* what makes you happy? The obvious answer for many of us is perhaps yes. How is happiness manifested? What does the outcome of happiness look like? This is a difficult question to answer because in history, people who seem happy, who "have it all," are typically only superficially happy.

Contentment stems from the types of thoughts we create individually; these are our internalized truths. And if our truths are false, we can never be happy. Happiness stems from mastering yourself with thoughts that evoke inner balance and harmony. It is the ability to create the reality appropriate for you.

We cannot live in a reality that someone else has created for them self. When we enviously emulate others or desire what they have, we cannot attain self-mastery. How can we self-master from another's stance or reality when individual realities are so unique? When we become immersed with jealous thoughts, it secludes us and reduces our ability for self-mastery, because we want their reality for ourselves. This is a dangerous path. Of course, there are many role models, people we respect in our lives, people

we aspire to emulate, and this is not what I refer to here. Instead, I speak of the jealous yearning and constant thoughts of comparison of our self with others. This creates a self-destructive path and gradually moves us farther away from the ability for self-mastery. Individuals who turn to drugs and alcohol from emotional turmoil may lose the ability to help themselves. The measures help to momentarily forget and silence the pain. With the practice of self-mastery, we can cope better with the pressures of life; it is my hope that with the practice of self-mastery, can make decisions that create a positive existence and be inspired by the most important role model, your Self.

Be Inspired by You

Humans have a constant need to seek inspiration. We recite inspirational and motivational sayings, poems, books, we listen to speakers and preachers. Inspiration is sought after in all directions, but rarely do we seek to be inspired by our perceptive being. Looking outward assumes we are not capable of inspiring our self, and we are. Certainly, others can enlighten us, but with the practice of self-mastery we depend less on them and more on our self for motivation. We take our self to task and retain responsibility. What inspires you about who you are? Where are you going in your life? What are you proud of? The answers to the questions may well be found in the motivation that stems from self-mastery.

Negative Exchanges Nurture Self-Mastery

We often have the yearning to remove toxic people from our lives. After all, we are told from childhood to be nice to others and avoid the people and situations that make us feel bad. Situations vary, and while individuals may choose to remove the self from a toxic circumstance, others might have limited choices. Imagine going to work every day to an irate supervisor. Over time, this can affect your mental, physical, and emotional health. However, you are employed and must endure the situation due to a lack of choice or work opportunities.

Frustration can escalate negative feelings. On a daily basis, we are all faced with tense moments; it could be a two-second glance or a one-hour meeting. As humans, we try to avoid these situations, but it is also in these moments that we can have powerful opportunities for self-mastery. When we move beyond negativities or create strategies for managing these situations or learn to "deal" with toxic people, we are inadvertently self-mastering.

Self-Prototype

Moments of adversity create in our minds templates for managing disquieting times. By managing these situations, we are better prepared to deal with similar situations or people in the future. The templates stick with us because we tend to recoil to them. This is especially critical in the corporate and business world. In the dense corporate environment, we find many dynamic personalities, so conflict is inevitable. Positive exchanges,

like the negative ones, allow us to deduce templates of recall. Placement in similar situations enables the reaffirmation of either feel-good or feel-bad moments. Self-mastery brings to the forefront awareness of the *ways* we deal with situations. The point is not if we are more effective than the other in an exchange, it is about being aware that certain situations will provoke more or less sensitivity.

Henceforth, the template patterns the way we practice and master our emotions as we move through life. For example, if newly learning to play a musical instrument, we must place the instrument in certain ways that might feel awkward at first. As we master playing the instrument, the awkward feel of the positioning disappears. If we struggle initially with a situation, we pay attention to doing it correctly, once we realize how much better it is in the correct form. Self-mastery acts the same way upon us. When confronted with a similar kind of situation, the archetype we have in mind is tweaked accordingly. Increasingly we become more effective at managing the negative (and positive) dimensions of our life.

Thus, one must pay conscientious attention to various types of interactions, because it is in these moments we foster self-esteem. We need to taste the bitter to appreciate the sweet. We tend to ruminate on the negativities in our lives: is the glass half full, or half empty? Depending on our meanings, we inextricably define and link a situation to by the previous patterns already formed. Because negative experiences impact us strongly, we must pay attention to how we cope.

Coping mechanisms are a direct result of self-mastery. With age, we may cope better only because we have experience and practice. However, times spent alone, reflecting on experiences, are powerful moments for telling us who we truly are. Ask yourself about the feelings, the reactions, the anxiety, the embarrassment caused by toxic moments. The responsibility of your own action is the most important element in a toxic situation. We can control our self but not others. We must be responsible and ask our self, what could I have done by moving the responsibility from them to myself? In this way we do not project our weakness, we embrace it.

While isolating oneself from the rest of the world is not an option for most of us, there is much to learn from the Dalai Lama's teachings. Self-mastery can be practiced through meditation. To disconnect from the material world and create inner peace enlivens self-mastery; the feel of each breath during meditation leaves no choice but to pay utter and infallible attention to the self.

Meditation allows the flow of heedful thoughts and awareness. In daily life, we must create outlets which nurture good practices. Search out your state of solitude, for it will create a wiser, stronger, and more peaceful persona. The distinct feature of self-mastery is it not only allows us to flourish, but it strengthens our interactions. The people we interact with will also thrive.

A distinct feature of modern and post-modern society is the myriad and vast amount of interactions we have. In a given day, we can interact with numerous colleagues, friends, acquaintances, superiors, family, children, educators, politicians, or medical professionals. In a typical day for me, I may interact with six hundred different people in a professional and personal capacity, depending on how many lectures I must give. Additionally, social media, Internet, Instagram, Twitter, Facebook add to our interconnectedness from afar.

With the practice of self-mastery, our interactions become less strenuous. We connect with others with more sincerity. We all know rich connections create positivity, and I contrast this with what is commonly known as "small talk." Instead, deep contacts with appreciation stem from an interest in the other. We may interact with individuals we deem as "insignificant." For example, a homeless person on the street may do or say something polite as we walk by. We think of that short connection and appreciate their comment or gesture. Perhaps the homeless person made our day by simply reinforcing the realization that if we have a home, we are fortunate; we may realize how lucky we are just to be alive, and this is self-mastery in practice. We do not seek out the big features of money and power, material possessions and economic success to feel prosperous. Instead, the small, seemingly insignificant actions and interactions with others create a positive template in our lives; a template that fosters empathy and further helps us to see things from others' perspectives.

Sociologists agree the Self is created based on the feedback we attain from others. This notion must begin with interaction. If we treat our self with dignity, create moments that move us toward self-mastery, we internalize thoughts such as "I am worthwhile, I respect me." Positive thoughts are the first step.

Secondly, we must master those internalizations adequately through continual reminders and actions. Our actions must be created and recreated. I was presented with an orchid plant in my home, and I speak to it often. I know that I cannot forget to nurture the plant continually, for this is the only way it will thrive. As humans, we often forget this. Self-mastery cannot be practiced monthly or weekly or on an annual vacation. It must be a part of our existence and presence ceaselessly.

In mastering ourselves, we gain a fruitful strength and stamina to deal with negative experiences. Self-mastery allows for movement beyond negative messages, rather than fixate on them. It frees us so that we focus on our positive virtues. For example, confidence cannot exist unless an individual is fully able to articulate it. Pretense of authenticity is just that, and our true persona will always surface. When we feel valued, we believe in our existence, we know that we are not surface material. Today, the selfie can be defined from various trajectories, it can be a surface-laden show of what we are externally, or it can communicate deep passion about something.

The Mature Self

Self-mastery has to occur first for us to lead a robust and positive life. The Self matures in moments of self-mastery. Age defies mastery. Surely, as we age we become wiser; this is the expectation. Perhaps the aging process is linear. But self-mastery is not a linear undertaking. It is more like the graph of a cardiogram.

Acting with grace and slow reactivity aids self-mastery. Taking time to think before we speak can powerfully aid in self-mastery because we contemplate before acting and communicating. The spoken word is never reverted.

Today, women are torn between work, professional activities, pursuit of education, and motherhood. Rarely are we expected to take time for ourselves. If we do, there is a sense of guilt. The task of nurturing, giving, loving are tasks we deem as duties. We master these well. We create this existence with our actions, so we must recreate it with action as well. We are distracted from our self to nurture, listen, support others, often more than we should, place our emphasis on the other sacrificing our own needs. This is a distraction away from our inner sensibilities. Once we have walked far away from the self, it becomes difficult to regain control.

The Fit Mind

People with heightened levels of self-awareness resonate with an aura, an allure that often seems mysterious. Why? Because there are so few of them in our

247

midst, we gravitate to these persons for the awareness they have for others in their present state. Rather than nurturing our own self, we often attach ourselves to these charming personalities. The point here is to show that we can create the same aura for our self and these exceptional dispositions should, in fact, inspire us to do the same. False confidence will only take one insofar as a true personality will inevitably surface.

Confident exuberance can only come from the ascending thoughts internalized at a deep level away from the abysmal surface interactions we conceive. A Harvard study that showed a young adult is likely to thrive with one close friend, rather than ten acquaintances, points to the quality rather than quantity of relationships.[xxviii] Today, we have many connections, people who we depend on for business, to help in our daily lives and the activities around work and personal commitments. The individuals are important to the practical workings of our lives. However, they do not take us to a deeper level in our relationships. Similarly, we compare the number of likes and followers we have on social media, and again, these are contacts that help to pass time and provide entertainment and amusement.

These interactions are important—we learn about the world, culture, politics from them—but they lack depth. Today, it seems that we spend most of our time connected to those moments of superficial exchanges. The time passes, then it is late or another event in our schedule beckons. Again, after the event, we check our status. The cycle continues, and we have placed connecting at a deeper level on the sidelines. Those interactions that are fulfilling or solitude for self-mastery become infrequent, even nonexistent. Taking its place are the more mundane surface-type associations. Surface interactions transcend to our sense of being negative because our understanding is laden on the surface.

Retaining friendships and connections is a challenge for working individuals and professionals. As a young mother, I found that my interactions were inconceivably on a basic level because my energies were limited to my children. When I began participating on social media, I felt an elation to connect with people similarly interested in the things I am passionate about, intellectual conversations, art, music, and writing. It was not long until I realized that in my busy day, the one hour or so that I had designated for "me" time in the evening was consumed with tweeting, liking, messaging, reconnecting and sharing.

Like most of us, I look forward to these connections because they make me feel alive and I value the relations I created with such wonderful people. I would never change this. However, I began to recognize that this "me" time I so dearly valued became rather erratic. Something was amiss. I felt connected, yet forsaken. I was consumed with the excitement of knowing what the day's activities and news events were. However, this was not enough. What happened with quiet reflection of the happenings in *my* day? I was no longer prioritizing personal reflection of the things that *really* mattered such as the big hugs from my

daughters when I arrived early, a rare occurrence, to pick them up after school, or the beautiful joy on the face of my girls as they ate a treat at Menchie's after a long day, or listening to them sing along to their favorite songs on the radio as we drove home. The realization that these moments came and went and I did not engage with them to appreciate how they strengthened my own sense of self was distressing.

I was not reflecting and valuing these experiences toward my own self-mastery. I was moved toward my surface connections more than finding the solitude for appreciation of the loveliest parts of my life. I was forsaking time to think about how important these moments are to me by doing other mundane activities. On the surface, it seems a situation that anyone could be placed in. We must prioritize moments for the conscious recognition of our opportunity toward self-mastery.

The mastery of you stems from believing in and trusting you to know you. I ask the questions often to my students: How important is it to know someone you care about? Do you spend as much time trying to know you as you do with others? In order to know you, you require clarity. Moments of mastery come with clarity of one's thoughts in order to process and comprehend a situation or person, whether in solitude or in company.

My passion for the English language is great. As a young girl, when most girls read fairy tales, I was interested in reading the *Concise Oxford English Dictionary*. I would leave my sisters as they played in the dollhouse and quietly make my way to the family library. To reach as high as I possibly could, I would stack cushions to stand on them. I used this technique to especially reach the second shelf that housed the dictionaries and thesauri, albeit in a wiggling unsteady manner.

One night, I found my father's cherished antique feather ink pen, and next to it was a full new bottle of blue ink. I felt lucky that the ink bottle was already open. I dipped the big feather stick into the bottle and pretended to write my name in the dictionary. Across the page, between the words, I wrote my name. I wanted to emulate the notes I saw my father make in the margins of the book. The oversize dictionary was bulky for my little hands. With excitement, as I tried to pull the dictionary closer to me, the full bottle of ink tipped over onto the open pages and kept flowing down to the ground onto the beautiful silk Persian carpet I sat on. My hands, the carpet, and the dictionary transformed to darkened shades of indigo. I was most upset about the dictionary, although I knew I that my parents would think otherwise. At this moment, rather than being worried about the event at hand, I realized the extent to which I was passionate about writing and reading. Ignoring the ink disaster, flipping past pages of blue, I sat happily reading. I had a world of words at my fingertips.

As most writers would agree, simplicity and clarity are the most powerful modes of conveying a writer's thoughts. For me, it was simple, minute experiences like this that nurtured a passion. Combined, they ignited a lifelong pursuit of writing. The stolen moments of writing and

reading had culminated to create me as I know me. In times of self-mastery, we recognize what we love and nurture those passions. Similarity, self-mastery should be practiced with the clarity of mind so that thoughts about you are not stifled. Despite my inked surroundings, I immersed myself in my passion that was to fulfill my sense of self-worth.

Chapter Eight
The Kindness Revolution
Narcissism and Self-Mastery: I Reside in Me

Solutions for self-mastery would include specialized workshops and seminars that I will be establishing. Along with these, there is yoga, breathing exercises, and the practical measured steps I discuss below.

Reflection is an important part of self-mastery. How do we come to terms with tragedy or appreciate the good things in our lives? Alone, we think and appreciate, we take time out to appreciate what we have and change what is toxic, and plan for where we want to be going.

Why is it that a cottage getaway for a weekend is so refreshing? We tune out by displacing the physical self from the business of daily life. Often, we request time to think about big decisions we must make such as buying a car, home, phone, or even which restaurant to dine at. We want the time so that we may reflect on all dimensions of the situation, decision, or purchase. How often do we set time aside to think about our *"me?"*

What does it take to effectively and practically apply self-mastery to our lives?

Actually, it is quite simple—no expensive equipment, gym, or objects required. Solitude and a special place, whether it is in our home, our office, a park, a side street, a quiet library, a church, or anywhere that gives a sense of peace and solace is appropriate for self-mastery.

Steal Your Moments

It is important to recognize that quiet plenitudes, while seeming the norm for promoting mindfulness, are only one mode of self-mastery. Certainly, self-mastery can be attained in the most unassuming environments as well. At a rock concert, a pop concert, a noisy restaurant, waiting for the green light at a red light, on vacation in the mountains, on the beach, on a hike, or on a boat, we can always own an opportunity for self-mastery. We just have to make it happen.

For example, I took my girls to their first Taylor Swift concert in May of 2015. In the midst of all the noise, excitement, screaming, cheering—just for a few moments, I tuned out, I disengaged with them, and engaged with me. I realized that the joy on my children's face and the fun my husband and I were having with them was all that mattered. In that moment, seeing them happy, healthy, and appreciating life was a beautiful moment. However, I felt good about me deeply as I thought about our life in that moment. I did not steal the moment in silence; it was begotten in a crowd-filled theater of thousands. To me this was powerful.

Ways to Find Everyday Solitude

In the most mundane activity of a given day, you can practice self-mastery. Sitting at your kitchen island, you may think aimlessly, blankly about *you*. Ask yourself, what is good or bad in your day? What motivates you? What are you most thankful for today? Whatever it is, bring it back to *you*, think that *you* are thankful to *you* because *you* created this reality for *you*. This is the foundation of self-mastery.

You may have a wonderful mentor, but your achievements, hard work, motivation, and ruthless perseverance happen because of you and the rest are support. This is empowering. Conversely, when we are having a bad day, we may self-blame. While it may be difficult in trying times to keep a positive mind, we must reconstitute the self to think of the positive things we have and *are*. We are all something good.

For women especially, we must recognize our value. I try to remember every day that I am grateful for my girls; they are kind, well-adjusted children because I am a good mother. Now this is not to say I endow myself with all credit, but self-mastery is about self-appreciation, so you are focused on what you are doing correctly. As I have demonstrated, once you achieve this focus, your children and anyone else are positively affected.

Self-Complementarity and Self-Criticism
Ten Ways to Deny Yourself of Self-Mastery

1. Not setting aside twenty minutes for "you" each day.

2. You worry about feeling selfish in moments of "you."

3. Not getting enough self-care in the form of exercise, sleep, and eating well.

is to come in the day. Not everyone may have the schedule to do this morning routine, but the point is not the particular time of day, it is the idea of finding the time that works for you with unrestrained inspection. For me, it was the morning with few moment of peace as I sip my coffee in silence and take deep breaths.

Simply learning to separate self from all else by the process of learning about yourself is a powerful tool of inner realization. Learning these techniques is a great beginning. Self-mastery is demonstrated in isolation and creates effectiveness in interactions for you, the individual.

Moving Beyond the Stigma of Boredom

Why do we require solitude? Unfortunately, our mechanically driven, ultra-productive society has created the assumption that alone time is selfish and unproductive. After all, we are told to spend time volunteering, helping the less fortunate, etc. Of course, these are important parts of our life; social activities allow our empathetic self to be reenacted. However, we must put our Self first, and this means to place emphasis on our needs, and once aspired, we can help others.

Because we value social facility, we seek to be sociable which is important, but we must respect that much of society is less social, or introverted. In fact, the research shows that constant sociability could be a way of hiding low self-esteem and a weak sense of self. Why? The idea is that constantly social beings require legitimation of others; hence, they seek them out persistently. Obviously this is

not the case for everyone, and the idea is to maintain balance. To be overly social or isolated means that other parts of our life suffer. We assume overly social individuals are not lonely, when in fact they may be quite isolated. The search for recognition enforces the notion that the individual themselves is unable to create happiness with the self, and this is self-destructive behavior.

Ultimately, I have deduced self-mastery to the following:

Sincerity to your being.

Empathy for you and others.

Lucidity of thought.

Foresight, forethought, foreshadow your behavior.

Manifestation of self is power.

Authentic self arises by attention to you

Simplicity in thought, word, and deed.

Transcend your positive energy to others.

Enhance your life and those you care for.

Reward yourself with the understanding of you.

Yield empathy for you, your loved ones, and humanity.

Self-Respect, Self-Fascination

Self-mastery triggers your self-interest. You must be fascinated with yourself, otherwise how can you expect others to find you interesting? This sparks your conscious sense of self-worth, which draws others in. Whether we achieve self-mastery for work or personal relationships, self-mastery guides us to be the best Self we have within us to be.

Selfishness is created when we do not take the time to enliven with our own being, and the result is self-disrespect. As the saying goes, if you do not respect yourself, how can you expect others to respect you? We treat others how to treat us.

What should resonate with the words here is that self-awareness is not developed. You always had it, and it only requires nurturance. I do not present any skill here that is unattainable, you already own the self. I am merely presenting the strategies. In fact, your willpower to step away and selfishly nurture your own self-worth is the most unselfish thing you can do.

Moments of self-mastery are when you disconnect from the roles and connect with the role of you. This is the only vehicle for self-worth.

Our lives are in pursuit of the roles defining what we are. I spend my days tending to my imaginary garden of roles: mother, wife, professor, colleague, friend, daughter, confidant, society member, and lecturer. The list is exhaustive. In reality, my being is the totality of all these facets that are me. At times I feel fragmented, and I must shift gears from being "Mom" at 7 a.m., to being "Professor" at 9 a.m. This switching of gears is exhausting. During one of my classes, I told the personal story about the pressures of being a mom and career woman. Within half an hour after a class, I move from being a revered professor and lecturer to "Mama." As I walk in my front door, I transform myself, my notes and briefcase swiftly placed down on the white marble floor, I am welcomed with my two angels yelling as I walk in, cheerios, puzzle pieces, Lego blocks create my pathway from the front door to kitchen. One hour later, I am still in my work suit, at the counter preparing dinner. I look at the clock. It is 11 p.m. As I walk up the winding iron staircase, I realize I "forgot" to have dinner.

Self-mastery will empower you to a self-awareness that you have always had. I am not doing or giving you any skill that you do not already own. No, I am merely presenting the strategies needed. In fact, your willpower to step away and selfishly nurture your own self-worth is the most unselfish act of all.

Perhaps you are a successful corporate executive or a first-time mother, or you are in the midst of a mid-life crisis, regardless of your place in society, the days are spent creating fulfillment for the *what* you are feature of your identity. These roles consume us, mother colleague, CEO, teacher, etc.

Self-mastery is about living life with self-interest and a conscious sense of self-worth. A strong Self can only thrive from self-mastery. When we take time for moments of solitude, from being what we are, we are practicing self-mastery because we move our focus to connect to who we are, to our sentient being, to our Self.

Whether we achieve self-mastery for work or personal relationships, self-mastery guides us to be the best Self we have within us to be.

Caving in to vulnerability was never a choice I gave myself. In proving to myself I could be all my roles without

reaching in toward me was self-defeating, and slowly tore
at my spirit.

Reconstitute the Self

Time for solitude for adults, professionals, and
children is vital. A source of inspiration for me is the word
atom, meaning indivisible of parts. Ironically, it is the
Sanskrit meaning of my name, "Renu." The mastery of you
propels an understanding that *you* exist as a whole entity.
An atom is indivisible of parts, and so too we must
recognize that as humans we are not fragmented. We are a
compendium of our thoughts. We carry an understanding of
who we are through reflective moments of self-mastery.

The calm of solitude inspires self-mastery and uplifts
us. For self-mastery to thrive, we must move away from
overt distraction, so that even in flashes of quiet, in the
midst of business, rattling of fans, pulses of keyboards,
voices on the television, clanging of dishes, chiming of new
message notifications, fury of indifference, blaring of a
street corner, vigour of engines, or the internal voice saying
"I should be productive instead of perceptive," we must
find time for the practice of self-mastery.

Certainly, life has various noises that may lend to
uplifting of the practice. These are the buzzing of the bees,
the crackle of tree branches in the wind, twigs breaking
under our feet, the crunch of crisp orange-hued autumn
leaves, the aired movement of dewdrops upon a windshield,
the sparkling sunlight on a bright day, in the background
the playful scream of a child, outside, unafraid, bareness of

footprints in hushed white sand, the chill of the winter air, a second hand indicating the welting of the hours as they float by, the beauty of a blossoming bud, right before your eyes, the nuance of your breath, the desire in a wish, the vibrant vicissitude of your thoughts, letting them float, to where they want to go, unfettered by anything or anyone. This is free will. This is self-mastery.

A child who is taught the importance of self-mastery at a young age will have an advanced template for future success. Such a model, from early on, creates a well-grounded adult. Today, rampant bullying could be due in part to the lack of solitude children experience. Technology and self-serving actions of the tech-savvy child do not uplift. Rather, the lack of solitude and face-to-face interactions may well be damaging to the internal Self. Most vulnerable are our children.

This is not to create the illusion that independent solace is the only necessity for emotional health. On the contrary, solitude allows a deep-seated strength to grow *and* that impacts our relationships positively. With a solid state of mind, we *want* to interact, we thrive interpersonally because we are more aware of our emotions and nurture self-control. What this means is we become more patient and understanding toward the other. Interactions become enjoyable rather than merely tepid or functional.

When quiet time is nurtured, we can focus on taken-for-granted parts of our Self. To pay attention to one's breath, giving utter infallible attention to the air in your being. Strategies such as meditation and mindfulness create

an awareness that is peaceful. In our busy lives, such solitary practice to focus on the intricate part of our life is difficult to set aside. However, when we make time, we create a pathway for effective interactions, laden in empathy. This is the distinct feature of self-mastery. Hence, self-mastery leads to a powerful humility that you did not know you were capable of. It becomes the power source for all you do. Self-mastery begets power. The beauty of self-mastery is it serves everyone else, but most importantly it serves you first. At times, it is the most broken and detached moments of our existence that self-mastery can flourish. It is such moments that require we self-focus, but these are precisely the moments that we self-ignore or try to forget.

To act with grace is to react with a thoughtful pause.

One must be selfish to be empathetic. Empathy is not about selflessness, it is not about self-sacrifice. On the contrary, people become empathetic due to a self-imposed desire to harness their need to obtain self-confidence by way of self-mastery. For example, an individual who practices self-mastery, gains stronger confidence and an advanced ability to place themselves in the other's shoes. Why? It is quite simple if we think about it; how can we give attention to *anyone* if we do not give attention to our Self first? The mind of the awkward and the power of silence or anything that sits on the margins of our society is where the optimal opportunities for self-mastery reside.

When others do not conform, perhaps it is a form of strength, not weakness. They are able to live according to their own measures and have a wisdom-filled presence that they are comfortable with.

Self-mastery is a process; however, it does not need to be linear in nature. Its development relies on the events and platitudes of individual life. Being selfish creates a path toward knowing *you*. Then you are readily able to give the people you most care about, the best of you. Would you want others to give you less? You must have a conscious mindset, a personal force for the dedication to its attainment. The mindset for self-mastery must precede the act of self-mastery. For example, if you are preparing for a marathon, you cannot go out and run, expecting to do well without practice. You must contemplate your potential, your stamina, and build mental and physical strength. You must engage thoughts about your potential to complete the goal. A runner in this process prepares the mind and body by exercising and envisioning the goal. To take part in the marathon, actions such as buying proper shoes, selecting a coach, practice, exercise, eating healthy give purpose to the goal. These are the small steps that we hope will lead to victory, but even if we are not victorious, we have created a template, a mindset that to attain a goal, we require small wins. We will return to the template for future goals. This is success. The process and not the *win*, it is the motivation. Thus, in preparing the mind for self-mastery, mindfulness and awareness to do it are a must. We need to know our potential, and self-mastery benefits the process. Life is often motivated by disappointments and few successes. By the practice of self-mastery, we are readily able to face our disappointments and value and care for our triumphs.

The Mindset is the most Powerful Tool for Self-Mastery

Self-mastery is a powerful tool for success. When the power of you is unleashed, you become confident and balanced. There is a compelling humility that is subconsciously produced in the realms of self-mastery. Some of us may call it charm or appeal. A charming personality can draw us in, set us afire, and we admire the person. It is a characteristic personality trait, and merely draws people in toward you. In the case of self-mastery, the allure of you is not the trait itself, but there is a pathway *you* create that allows others to feel that *they* are valuable beings.

As humans, the capability factor is paramount insofar as we are naturally drawn toward people that make us feel worthy and energize our spirit. Often, we want to avoid "toxic" people or situations. Instead, look for that which will nurture our soul. We readily grasp at opportunities that enable us to feel a sense of worth.

With the sense of worth we gain, self-mastery gives rise to humility. We act with integrity and purpose. Feeling worthiness enables our energy to help others do the same. In fact, we treat and speak to people in a way that solidifies their state of being, not our own because we already know our value (the paradox of selfishness). Self-mastery moves

focus toward kindness. This does not become a chore, or require we espouse great energy. Rather, it flows naturally. When we have not attained self-mastery, placing emphasis on the other in our interactions becomes a tedious task because we are absorbed with our self only. These are the people we believe brag or talk about their achievements and nothing else. At the core of this is a lack of inner self-knowledge. Indeed, those who cannot appreciate the presence of others are enraptured in their own self precisely because they have not taken moments to practice self-mastery.

Kindness Requires No Orchestration

In fourth grade, I was chosen as one of four children in my entire junior school to receive lessons of a string instrument of choice. I chose the viola. Lessons were two times per week for the last thirty minutes of lunch. My music teacher was a short, young, and very pleasant freckle-faced British woman with an accompanying accent. I remember admiring the delicate gold stud earrings she always wore. I often pondered why she had a boy-cut hairstyle and wore only pants, while most of my other teachers were wearing frilly and floral frocks, bell bottom jump suits, tightly fitting pencil skirts, cowboy boots, sweaters draped over shoulders, and smelled of strong perfume. Often, hands were well manicured, and the nail color of choice was bright red. Although this was not too long ago, there was a level of innocence and kindness in the

halls of the schools, a niceness that seems to have faded today.

The teachers seemed so much happier and simple in demeanor. For a budding viola player, the obvious next step was to participate in the school orchestra and attend concerts and festivals across Canada. Only the most talented and promising students auditioned and made it to the school orchestra. Fortune smiled, and I joined the group. Perhaps one of the highlights of my life is playing Brandenburg Concerto No. 3, winning at the Kiwanis Festival.

Our concerts included pieces from *Annie*: "Tomorrow," "Bridge Over Troubled Water," "Send In the Clowns," and other beautiful classics.

I would awaken early on Tuesday, Thursday, and Friday morning at 6 a.m., and orchestra practice began at 7 a.m. If my father was free, he would drive me; otherwise, I would meet my friend, and she and I would walk to school. I recall the earliness of waking seemed eerie; too quiet for me to understand. As a young girl, these moments preceding the sun's appearance were sullen but sweet. Sometimes, we would be walking to school, and it would still be dark, especially if the clouds were overcast. My friend and I would reminisce about our excitement for the next orchestra trip. Between our still-tired laughter and deep tiresome breaths of having to wake too early, I would stare at the blackness of the sidewalk. In springtime, the concrete was often drenched with heavy rain. My yellow rubber rain boots would splash and wave to the ground as I walked on.

In winter, my hefty snow boots would transcend the heaviness of the snow, and we laughed as we made tracks in the freshly snowed paths. One good thing with being out so early: we were rewarded with being the first to stomp on the fresh meadows of snow. It seemed a celebration to be the first to walk through the perfect landscape, before anyone else. In summer, we would walk in more brightness than spring or winter. We would wear our running shoes, and we would try to play hopscotch as we skipped on our way toward the schoolyard.

Mrs. Gaston had recently become Mrs. Armbridge by marriage; she was our music teacher, and orchestra conductor. She was a middle-aged but young-looking, and we all wondered why she was not married, until she was. She was very attentive. She often wore beige lace blouses with long black skirts, and she had glasses and flowing bouncy shoulder-length hair that was a mix of blackish gray. When her hair was in big flowing loose curls, I knew it was a special occasion, like if we were playing a piece for the school's Friday morning assembly.

I would walk into practices, and the members of the orchestra would be lined up as she tuned all the instruments with a tuning box. This always astonished me, from violins to cellos, to bass, to violas; she just tuned all the instruments. I would look in amazement as she plucked the strings of the instruments, turning her ears east and west to hear the sounds resonate decorously. If any string was

broken, she would re-string our instruments in that moment and off we would go. Volunteers for the week would set up all of the members' podiums and our music sheets, we would sit in pairs, and the layout was that of a typical orchestra. Lines of violins, then violas, then cellos, and the bassists stood at the back of the collective.

Our next task was to tighten our bows made of silken horse hair and rub rosin in an up and down motion on the bow. The rosin was sticky and powdery, but I found it very relaxing to massage it on the silky smooth bow. All members would delicately rosin their bows big or small depending on the instrument, and we seemed to compete for having the best-rosined bow; whoever did would make the sweetest sounds resound from their instrument. We would then prepare for warm-up as the sweet senseless tunes of everyone warming up began to fade. We would begin with warm-ups, the music table in various tempos. At times I would watch as the more advanced viola players played in staccato, and I would wish I could do that.

One morning, a boy by the name of Michael saw me looking at him. After practice, he asked if I wanted to learn staccato, I said yes. Michael began playing violin years before and was the most dedicated and advanced player in the orchestra of about thirty members. He was also a talented artist, comics were his favorite, and he had the smallest, neatest handwriting I have ever seen.

The value of youthful interaction is very important, even today. Our numerous Kiwanis wins took us to Indianapolis as my school was part of an exchange

program. I recall a boy "falling in love with me." It was innocent, infatuation-type love, but I will never forget this time when interaction and nature collided; there was no barrier between us and those we communicated with. He sought my attention although he was the boy all girls giggled around. The last day of the trip, the students bid us farewell, and Frank spent a few moments saying "goodbye" to my friends and me. He gave me a white envelope and made me promise I would not open it until we were well on our way. As he stood watching, we loaded onto the bus, and I could see tears in his clear blue eyes from my window seat.

As the bus drove through the winding tree-lined road, lush with greenery, all I could think about was, why me, why was he so kind to me? He did not even know me well. My friend told me to open the envelope, and on the back SWAK was written. Too young to even know what that meant, I was puzzled. My friends told me it meant "sealed with a kiss." The obvious light-hearted playful teasing followed as the bus echoed with laughter about my letter. I felt a deep sadness, but I did not know why. I was confused by this unconditional kindness, and it made a deep impression. I realized that strangers so far apart could be kind and gentle to others they did not even know very well.

Since then, in my thirteen-year-old mind, I recognized that nothing could replace thoughtfulness, and I knew that these moments would stay with me. I realized that such acts of kindness are rare, and I decided that I wanted more kindness to exist. The kindness I refer to here is simply kindness *without* any reason, just as I had experienced. Self-mastery creates opportunities for unconditional acts of kindness. Being strong-willed and self-fulfilled, we can help others without any motive. We just do it. The world needs more of this and self-mastery can guide this practice.

I never saw him again, but his kindness stayed with me for the rest of my life. A human being's life and the value of existence has only one measure, kindness toward the other. Being a professor and lecturer has taught me much about kindness derived from my self-mastery.

Professors are an odd breed: We live in great contradictions and juxtapositions. We are to be hidden, isolated in our own towers of ivory or gray or ebony. We are to research, write in solitude. Then engage with anywhere from two to five hundred students for three hours. We become comedians, entertainers, scientists, artists, politicians, lawyers, parents, muses, role models, and yes, intellectuals, all to inspire our students. The old adage is the distinguished, sophisticated, suave intellectual, or the stereotypical "scientist" hairdo. We are supposedly endowed with wisdom and intelligence. However, this is only the beginning. As educators, we have the power to be kind, to treat students in a way that values their place in the world, regardless of where it may be. We instill knowledge and herein is our power. We can change the lives of students with kindness that brings forth their potential.

Being Cruel to Be Kind

Society, unfortunately, has equated being alone with self-centeredness. Today, we can agree, we must be "out there." Success follows the self-assured action, yet the irony is we are expected to gain these traits by becoming increasingly social and not seeking solitude. I render the opposite to be true. To become personable, we need to self-interact; how can others think positively about us if we do not know what our greatest strengths are? How can others want to be in our company if we do not value our own company? Personal and professional success is increasingly connected upon individual ingenuity and imagination. After all, those who are successful are the ones who took a chance, offered something different. And yet, this can only be inspired by originality and self-appraisal through solitary reflection and devoid of disturbance—in other words, by self-mastery.

We often look up to the person who is the social butterfly, one who has many friends, and we are inspired by them. It seems odd or even aberrant to be left with our own self, and others react with profound disappointment. However, we must use time alone to regroup and self-reference. The social butterfly may be a person everyone wants to be around. The person could be unhappy, and the continual social presentation of self breaks down the inner sense of self. Thus, the individual knows no other way to seek acceptance apart from looking for the connection with others. Of course, we all thrive and need friendships, and group interaction is paramount to emotional health. As a social scientist, I know this well. However, going the opposite direction to being immersed in all but your company could be expressively detrimental too.

Knowledge is power, but it can also serve to distort reality. With knowledge, we begin questioning everything. As a sociologist, I hyper-analyze endlessly, and at times do not enjoy my experiences for the sake of appreciating them. I soon realize that overthinking is detrimental to my health. I refer to this as the power of letting others be.

Do Not Take for Granted the Taken for Granted

The ways we communicate from the minutest gesture to an overt loud action always conveys something significant to others. We often take this for granted. As a wonderful professor of mine at the University of Toronto helped me to understand, there are many layers beneath the manifest actions we share. Meanings come to exist with centuries of life, longevity, and brevity. We term this as the actions that are "taken for granted." Indeed, we act daily from wake to sleep without paying much attention to the intent of our actions. Upon waking, almost unconsciously, we perform actions to prepare for the day. Like breathing, we do not think, "Now, I will take the next breath"—these actions are second nature. If these acts are second nature, what is our *first* nature?

The taken-for-granted dimensions of our existence imply we act without predetermination, especially when we are accustomed to and comfortable with something. Can you name people or places that make you feel utterly comforted? Are you comforted by you? What does that even mean? Taking something for granted, we ignore it, assume it is always present, pervasive. This is the way we come to treat our self without self-mastery. We lack appreciation for our own presence. We cannot do this. We cannot ignore the self, because it is the place where self-mastery takes precedence. As with a lively garden filled with colourful blooming roses and lush greenery, we must prune, and cut wildflowers and remove the weeds that detract from the beauteous magnificence. Similarly, with self-mastery, we become aware so that we may trim away the toxic elements from our lives. As the saying goes, a garden does not grow overnight, and as with our Self, this takes gradual and dedicated work. Over time, the fruit of our emotional labor toward our self reaps a powerfully positive consequence.

Self-mastery nurtures the emotional intelligence that we need to thrive. Our emotions are inadvertently connected to our sense of self. Knowing who we are internally gives expression to the external element of emotions. Emotions are a manifestation of our self-thoughts. Emotions are extrinsic. Self of self is intrinsic. Sense of self precedes and decides emotional output. Therefore, depending on how strong or weak your sense of self is, your emotions will produce the reactions to this sense of self. Certainly, some emotions are more powerful than others.

When we act impulsively, when we act in ways others do not understand, perhaps we need to step back and delve

deeper into self-mastery. Most of us have been confronted with a situation where someone tells us, "I don't understand you…anymore." When we act out of the normal range of our typical Self, often others see it more clearly than we ourselves do, and this is perhaps because we are consumed with a situation or present circumstance detracting us from our self. The paradox is most of us become distracted from our self in stressful times, but this is precisely the time that we must be focusing on our self. Many of us do not. Why? Because when we do not spend times of solitude to know our self deeper, we lose control outwardly; this is where others see the difference. We can become so immersed in a problem that we do not recognize changes in our personality, in our Self. This inward sense of weakness from stressful times is expressed outwardly and subconsciously.

At the heart of such a transformation, I embed empathetic understanding. Given the various modern-day ideologies that we abide by, I have provided a breakdown of different actions regarding empathy. The overarching lack of empathy in social life hinders self-mastery today. Most critically, we must use empathetic understanding, to enrich our lives and the lives of others. We must change our gaze, and this requires conscious contemplation. By doing so, we shift the gaze from *me* to *you*. We enrich each other's lives rather than merely tolerating each other's position or brand.

Self-Mastery, Self-Expression, and Narcissism

Self-mastery, as I have repeated throughout these pages, is a humble internal thought process that centers on your sentient being, without interference and stimulation from anyone but yourself.

I love social media, and like many people, I feel connected and thrive on the "feeling" of connection I retain when I communicate with people. However, narcissism could surface quickly if the constant connection with others is the only way that we center our time alone. Self-absorption in this context is materialistic; it espouses all your activities, everything you do to gain legitimation from others, the things you like, who you are dating, your friends, your kids, your home, car, etc. I think it is a wonderful thing to share. But these surface-oriented sharing of material aspects of our existence, while positive to certain degrees, can become problematic. I ponder how the pathways of our interactions have changed, and I observe that we as humans love attention, love to feel valued. But the means of grasping for such attention today is only on the surface, and this I argue intensifies narcissistic behavior. To constantly put our self out there, seeking the attention of others, we become narcissistic because we value their attention onto us, we seek more of it to the point where we value their attention of us more than we value the attention we give to our own self.

The problem with sharing all the outward experiences we have is that the significance of such experiences remains external to us. Sharing is a must for human

connections to flourish, and this is not to say we must not share our happiness. However, to simply share experiences and set them free for others to see and engage with, our experiences become about what others think more than what we think or learned from them. The result is we do not entertain a deep thought process about experiences, and if we do not sit silently and reflect upon them, we do not give our self a chance to learn from and understand our positive or negative experiences. We often say someone commits a mistake repeatedly and this leads to a relationship breakdown, addiction, etc. We must ask why these actions repeat themselves. Lacking self-mastery can be related to addictive and destructive behavior.

Self-mastery is about self-absorption, but not an obsessive one as in the case of the narcissist. Narcissism breeds vanity, egoism, conceit, pride, arrogance, smugness, selfishness, and insecurity. Self-focus happens for the *wrong* reasons. Self-mastery conversely breeds selflessness, generosity, kindness, compassion, empathy, and security. We self-focus for the right reasons. Deep self-thought enables the evaluation of our self and has an intense effect on our self-respect. Take solace in you and you will prevail; we are born alone and will die and return alone.

Discernment of the self occurs in moments of self-mastery and leads to a fulfilling existence. The importance of alone time is that such loneliness allows observation without distraction. How often is it that we observe a coworker or individual who has a skill that we are trying to

master? We pay keen attention, write notes, observe, and record important points. When was the last time that you recorded an observation about a strength or weakness of yours? Writing in a diary allows for individuals to capture thoughts and feelings about daily events. Self-mastery is nuanced differently because it involves a deeper reflection than those about events and the ways they made us feel. Most importantly, *we focus on our strengths and weaknesses we discovered about ourselves during the time the event occurred.*

Today, social connections are a practical and resourceful tool for eliciting reaction and feedback from hundreds, thousands, even millions of "followers." Does having six million likes for a picture we posted translate to a deep sense of self? Indeed, this can be a lonely place, while we care about how our actions affect others and touch them personally. The problem with this is that the connection is a base and materialistic one. It lacks depth, and the fulfillment is momentary.

We then challenge the mundane with yet another action beckoning for attention. Instead of focusing on our Self in solitude, or connecting with the "me," we continue to relish and seek the input and opinions of others. While it is important to present our self in a positive light, and certainly these activities drive success and recognition, connection and networks, we must realize a balanced approach is required. Seeking to connect with many others is not the same as deeply connecting with you.

In fact, seeking out others can become a negating dimension of our existence. Often we note this as "caring about what others think." In the process, we convince ourself to believe that our thoughts of "me" are contingent upon others. If we think of the people we consider successful or who we admire—sport stars, scientists, Nobel Prize winners—they are often the individuals who were originally ridiculed or pursued their cause, or belief, in spite of what others thought. These are the individuals with a powerful drive which ultimately connects to the strong sense of self they possessed. Without inner strength, they would not have pursued their cause.

Self-Mastery for Professional Fulfillment

My professional passion lies with lecturing and instruction. I may make a point in my lecture, and I hear pin-drop silence in the hall of three hundred students. The whimsical silence is profound.

Telling. It is a silence diluted with thoughtful machinations.

Shuffling. Silence again.

I realize the silence is unique. I have made my students think; I can hear and see them thinking. In this silence, my own self-mastery is uplifted, and I selfishly internalize the high. My story struck a chord. The silence declares victory, devoid of computer keyboards clicking, classmates whispering, cell phones ringing, text messages radiating with ripples, pens and pencils clicking and pulsing. Even the whirring of the fan on my console is silenced. I stand on the podium and consume the moment. Impressed upon me, I realize my power to touch the lives of so many. My power to lead them in the right direction, a direction devoid of actual power; a pure compassion, a compassion that leads this silence. To let them know they matter. I realize I could not have this effect had I not nurtured my own sense of self. My own self-mastery and the confidence it gives me allows me to positively touch their lives.

Self-mastery takes the power that you have and enhances your control over your thoughts so that they are centered on you. Giving this brainpower to your inner you rather than ruminating on a stressful workday for even twenty minutes of your day redirects your energy and channels it to flow toward you, not away from you. When we fixate on the negatives of a day, your power is wasted outwardly to a situation beyond you. Exuding this power externally does nothing for personal fulfillment. This energy is wasted outwardly to a place undeserving of your energy.

Forgiveness from things you regret is an important dimension of the self-mastery process. Regret, remorse, and guilt are self-destructive and fester in a self-debilitating circularity. Grace that is poised toward the self, uplifts positive sentiments. Self-mastery allows us to conceive of our remorseful thought. Positive experiences, as well as making mistakes, enliven self-mastery. Regret and fixation on our mistakes reel complacency. Regret places us on a wrong path, but the realization of the mistake is a powerful tool of self-discovery. This realization is powerful because

it enables us to stay true to our values, and the mistake reinforces actions and events we *do not* want to experience.

Mastery of you allows you to occupy your mind with thoughts of you. For but twenty minutes, you take control and put full focus on you. You may pause, stop giving to others, the attention reverts inward. Do you not deserve twenty minutes to you each day? Over time I can say that this becomes addictive. I speak from personal experience, and after this practice, I felt a positive turn in my life. It was my purpose to share these thoughts, especially for women who give to their work, families, and children. We need to get the message across that it is important to pay attention to alone time.

How much of your day is spent on making decisions, regretting decisions? It is wonderful to receive accolades for our personal and professional achievements, but are these achievements about you? Does the input of another make the achievement more or less important? If you are consumed with impressing or showing your ability to another, it is not a pure achievement. It is less about you. This is the paradox of achievement, and often we want recognition from others when we achieve, but ultimately the achievement should be about self-recognition first. Spending time alone knowing you is the best way to nurture effective interaction skills. We build resilience.

Seeing our self positively as in "the looking-glass self" alleviates the tendency to internalize negative reactions, and we effectively transcend them. This is not to say that our interactions depend on others' reactions only, but

negative reactions, which we often fixate on, become better dealt with; we attain effective tools. Low self-esteem results when we place importance on negative energies. We compare and contrast to the point of self-destruction.

Your ability to master yourself and control events in your life leads to a positive notion of where you are and where you stand in life. Self-mastery is about self–control; often those who are not in control are told to seek the help of professionals, precisely because they lack control. In contrast, the more successful an individual is, the more they may seek out help to better themselves.

Finally, all self-mastery pathways must be uniquely driven because we are all distinctive individuals, but we are equal in our humanity and potential to reach for kindness. Materialism and privilege can support self-mastery, but it cannot propel it—only you have that power. I wish you the best as you walk the path of understanding the greatest entity of all: you.

How can I know to love you, if I do not love myself first?

–Renu Persaud

Acknowledgments

It would be an injustice to attempt to display gratitude to many within the confines of words and space here.

Thus, I wish to thank all of you, who know who you are for your cherished support and unrelenting enthusiasm for his undertaking and, most importantly, for me.

In particular, I had the great fortune to work with professionals who are the best in their respective fields in North America and abroad. From my publicist and agent, cover designer, web designer, local and international news professionals, and media outlets, to my editors, copyeditors, and fact-checker, journalists, columnists, book critics, screenplay writers, directors, book reviewers, bloggers, a Supreme Court judge, poets, sponsors, colleagues, the University of Toronto, OISE/UT, the University of Windsor, the Provost, and affiliates at Columbia University, my colleagues at Harvard University, and Duke University: the message of my book is owed to your support.

At the onset of writing my book, it was repeatedly noted how difficult it is to obtain blurbs and reviews for newer writers. I hoped for even one blurb. I received forty from highly regarded and notable writers and professionals at the pinnacle of their respective fields. I am indebted and humbled by all of you who saw the depth and potential of this important work. Thank you with all my heart and soul.

To my parents Pundit Chidanand and Raynuka Sharma, thank you for your love. Knowing I am your pride and joy has motivated me beyond reasoning.

To my husband David, you are the invisible, silent strength of me. As you stand by allowing me to dream, you seek not gratitude or recognition, all the while protecting me.

Finally, to my beautiful daughters, Sarah and Emma, it is through your presence my Self was awakened.

Author Biography

Renu S Persaud is an accomplished Canadian social scientist, professor, lecturer and author. With a BA, MA and PhD from the University of Toronto, her ideas and adept understanding of social life have touched the lives of thousands of individuals. She is actively involved in research and writing on sense of self, well-being and mending of the broken spirit.

Index

alone time, 41, 43, 64, 76, 123, 181, 197, 237, 268, 288, 292

audacity, 166, 212, 217, 218, 219, 220, 222, 228

authenticity, 91, 93, 135, 228, 258

backstage, 69, 70, 72, 73, 74

consciousness, 14, 80, 95, 96, 97, 102, 103, 114, 251

contemplate, 8, 41, 57, 63, 71, 120, 178, 200, 202, 225, 247, 258, 276

creativity, 116, 117, 118, 150, 152, 165, 196

effective montage, 96

emotional intelligence, 285

Emotional intelligence, 72

Emotional Quotient, 186

front stage, 41, 69, 70, 72, 73, 74, 75

graciousness, 129

Intelligence Quotient, 186

intentional process, 68

Internet, 32, 74, 133, 240, 256

jealousy, 108, 109, 187

mindfulness, 95, 150, 167, 223, 265, 274, 276

Paradox of Selfishness, 7, 66

roaring whispers, 172, 208, 235

self-absorbed, 53, 56, 64, 120, 168, 224, 225, 233

self-belief, 85, 173

Self-control, 102, 103, 124, 125, 211, 267, 274

self-destructive, 15, 95, 139, 224, 225, 252, 269, 291

self-fulfilling prophecy, 107

self-immersion, 30, 225

Self-importance, 60, 71, 114, 126, 127, 128, 129, 142, 144, 161, 162, 165, 239

selfishness, 45, 47, 53, 67, 68, 74, 75, 86, 91, 120, 168, 183, 277, 288

self-knowledge, 30, 44, 94, 277

selflessness, 45, 47, 66, 75, 91, 157, 275, 288
self-pyramid, 129
self-reflection, 116, 149
self-regard, 41
self-respect, 31, 93, 133, 217, 228, 288
self-sacrifice, 28, 53, 88, 100, 101, 154, 275
self-time, 43, 197
self-worth, 8, 29, 31, 33, 52, 53, 59, 61, 68, 73, 74, 77,
81, 82, 87, 88, 92, 93, 104, 106, 114, 116, 118, 122, 144,
166, 170, 192, 196, 197, 198, 201, 209, 213, 220, 231,
235, 236, 239, 240, 243, 244, 263, 270, 271, 272
Social Interaction Quotient, 186
sociology, 32, 95, 107, 110, 147, 163, 189
solitude, 29, 37, 38, 42, 48, 54, 57, 58, 59, 61, 62, 63, 70,
74, 77, 80, 116, 119, 123, 156, 165, 195, 196, 197, 216,
229, 230, 237, 249, 256, 260, 261, 262, 267, 268, 272,
273, 274, 282, 283, 286, 289
spirit-injury, 139
suffering, 17, 23, 45, 50, 57, 116, 124
suicide, 161, 162
thoughtfulness, 79, 91, 98, 143, 282
two-way dynamic, 69
well-being, 45, 67, 88, 91, 133, 141, 186, 190, 215
Win, the, 140, 168, 292

[i] Cain, Susan. *Quiet: The Power of Introverts in a World That Can't Stop Talking*. New York: Broadway Books, 2013.

[ii] Swaminathan, Nikhil. "What Predicts Grad School Success?" American Psychological Association. September 2012. http://www.apa.org/gradpsych/2012/09/cover-success.aspx.

[iii] Pike, Alison, and Thalia C. Eley. "Links between Parenting and Extra-familial Relationships: Nature or Nurture?" *Journal of Adolescence* 32, no. 3 (2009): 519-33.

[iv] Goffman, Erving. *The Presentation of Self in Everyday Life*. Garden City, NY: Doubleday, 1959.

[v] Cuddy, Amy J.C., Caroline A. Wilmuth, and Dana R. Carney. "The Benefit of Power Posing Before a High-Stakes Social Evaluation." Harvard Business School Working Paper, No. 13-027, September 2012.

[vi] Cain, Susan. *Quiet: The Power of Introverts in a World That Can't Stop Talking*. New York: Broadway Books, 2013.

[vii] Salerno, Steve. *SHAM: How the Self-help Movement Made America Helpless*. New York: Crown Publishers, 2005.

[viii] Mead, George Herbert, and Charles William Morris. *Mind, Self, and Society from the Standpoint of a Social Behaviorist*. Chicago, IL: University of Chicago Press, 1962.

[ix] Dewey, John. *Art as Experience*. New York: Minton, Balch & Company, 1934.

[x] Mills, C. Wright. *The Sociological Imagination*. New York: Oxford University Press, 1959.

[xi] Carnegie, Dale, Dorothy Carnegie, and Arthur R. Pell. *How to Win Friends and Influence People*. New York: Simon and Schuster, 1981.

[xii] Carnegie, Dale, Dorothy Carnegie, and Arthur R. Pell. *How to Win Friends and Influence People*. New York: Simon and Schuster, 1981.

[xiii] Weber, Max. *The Protestant Ethic and the Spirit of Capitalism*. New York: Scribner, 1958.

[xiv] Durkheim, Émile, Steven Lukes, and W. D. Halls. *The Division of Labour in Society*. Basingstoke: Palgrave Macmillan, 2013.

[xv] Durkheim, Émile, Steven Lukes, and W. D. Halls. *The Division of Labour in Society*. Basingstoke: Palgrave Macmillan, 2013.

[xvi] Durkheim, Émile, Sarah A. Solovay, John Henry Mueller, and George Edward Gordon Catlin. *The Rules of Sociological Method*. New York: Free Press of Glencoe, 1964.

[xvii] Durkheim, Émile. *Suicide, a Study in Sociology*. Glencoe, IL: Free Press, 1951.

[xviii] Dewey, John. *Art as Experience*. New York: Minton, Balch & Company, 1934.

[xix] McIntyre, Lisa J. *The Practical Skeptic: Core Concepts in Sociology*. Boston: McGraw-Hill Higher Education, 2006.

[xx] Krznaric, Roman. *Empathy: A Handbook for Revolution*. London: Rider Books, 2014.

[xxi] Durkheim, Émile. *Suicide, a Study in Sociology*. Glencoe, IL: Free Press, 1951.

[xxii] Weber, Max. *The Protestant Ethic and the Spirit of Capitalism*. New York: Scribner, 1958.

[xxiii] McIntyre, Lisa J. *The Practical Skeptic: Core Concepts in Sociology*. Boston: McGraw-Hill Higher Education, 2006.

[xxiv] Mead, George Herbert, and Charles William Morris. *Mind, Self, and Society from the Standpoint of a Social Behaviorist*. Chicago, IL: University of Chicago Press, 1962.

[xxv] Blakemore, Sarah-Jayne. "Social-Cognitive Development during Adolescence." *Child Psychology and Psychiatry*, 2011, 62-66.

[xxvi] Bourdieu, Pierre. *Outline of a Theory of Practice*. Cambridge, U.K.: Cambridge University Press, 1977.

[xxvii]

[xxviii] Clark, D. M. T., N. J. Loxton, and S. J. Tobin. "Declining Loneliness Over Time: Evidence From American Colleges and High Schools." *Personality and Social Psychology Bulletin* 41, no. 1 (2014): 78-89.